HAUNTED
WEST END THEATRES

HAUNTED
WEST END
THEATRES

IAN JOHN SHILLITO & BECKY WALSH

INVESTIGATION PHOTOGRAPHY BY SANDY GOLDEN

The History Press

Front cover photography by Nina Rangoy

Frontispiece: *Ian and Becky ghost hunting at The Queens Theatre.*

First published in 2007 by Tempus Publishing

Reprinted in 2011 by
The History Press
The Mill, Brimscombe Port,
Stroud, Gloucestershire, GL5 2QG
www.thehistorypress.co.uk

British Library Cataloguing in Publication Data.
A catalogue record for this book is available from the British Library.

ISBN 978 0 7524 4521 2

Typesetting and origination by
Tempus Publishing.
Printed and bound in England.

CONTENTS

ACKNOWLEDGEMENTS

Many thanks to everyone in the West End theatre community who has supplied us with stories and interviews. Without you, this book would not be possible.

Westminster Archives, Camden Library Local Studies and Research Centre, the Theatre Museum, Deborah Lean, Collette McEntree, John Chittenden and Ambassadors Theatre Group, Steve Pleasance, Sandy Golden, Mike Cordina, Lisa Dawson, Craig Russell, Matt Smith, Ed Douglas, Ned from the Old Vic, James Topping, Bill Smith, Chris Brooke, Sam Thurlby-Brooks, Shelly Debour, Nikki Hulme, Cathy O'Rourke, Jonathon and Chris at the Victoria Apollo box office, Susanna Mellows, William Ingrey, Lee Tasker, *Spirit and Destiny* magazine, Christina and Ed at Treadwell's bookshop, Juliet Rylance, Jo Hall, Sir Donald Sinden, Ruth Slaney-Abridge, Pete and Blair from the Aldwych, Dame Judi Dench, Linda Nichol, *Prediction* magazine, Ben Evans and Arron from the Trafalgar Studios, Steve Donald, Steve Parsons from Para Science and Dr Ciarán O'Keeffe for enlightenment, Yvette and Karl for the experience, Ben from Haunted Experience, Tom Polo, Sarah Guppy, Alistair Sutherland, Stephen Murturgh, William Byers, Tony at the Haymarket, Natalie Bloch, Chris Hawkins, Brian Connelly, all of Becky's students, Cheryl and the College of Psychic Studies, Suzy Jenvey, Sophie at MBA, all at Tempus.

INTRODUCTION

Both Ian John Shillito and Becky Walsh have been aware of their psychic abilities since childhood. Becky has been communicating with spirits ever since, yet Ian suppressed his ability, only to have a reawakening in his mid-thirties. Since the early 1990s, both Becky and Ian worked extensively in many of the capital's theatres. Even though the West End is a small community they had never met. Between them, their jobs ranged from followspot operator, fly man and stage crew but finally they both settled in stage management. At the turn of the millennium, the two independently realised they needed to branch out of the theatre world and follow their spiritual path. For a short while, their psychic awareness flourished alongside their theatrical careers. In late 2005 Becky and Ian met for the first time. Both have since left theatre and now work as professional psychics. Between them, the two appear in the media and press on a regular basis.

Ian has appeared on the hugely successful paranormal TV programme *Most Haunted* and presently runs the London Paranormal Society, offering public vigils in some of the capital's most haunted locations. Becky teaches at the respectable College of Psychic Studies and presents her own psychic show on London's ever popular LBC 97.3 FM radio station and regularly performs her one-woman The Stand Up Psychic Show.

Ian and Becky first worked together as stage managers at the Dominion Theatre in 2005. It was here that they decided to join forces on this project. The plan was to investigate the alleged ghost stories associated with West End theatres in a series of paranormal vigils. Ian decided to take on the role of paranormal investigator and Becky, the role of the psychic. Ian collated poignant and relative information about possible hauntings, searching for even the slightest essence of a story, whilst Becky tuned into her psychic ability, enhancing the story or eradicating the myth. They held vigil in dark auditoriums, lonely stairwells, and melancholy boxes, behind the scenery and underneath the stages in the search of the theatrical spirits. At a later stage, their findings were matched up to the validated history of London.

This is the first time a collection of theatrical ghost stories of this magnitude has been put together. Over recent years, many of the most famous theatres and their associated ghosts have been written about in depth, yet little is known about the smaller theatres and their spooky inhabitants. Are they haunted too? The historical sites upon which they all are built can certainly comprehend the possibility of a haunting. The combination of both Becky and Ian's personal interests in the psychic, the theatre and the paranormal was too much to ignore. They worked

London's theatre land is said to be riddled with ghosts.

solidly, knitting together fact and fiction, and separating the natural from the supernatural. Eight months later the book was finished. The result is a historical sweep through the paranormally active theatres of the West End. With literally hundreds of witness stories from actors, backstage and front-of-house staff, they reveal the most haunted theatres in London.

SYNOPSIS

London is said to be the most haunted city in the world and with over 2,000 years of habitation, it has certainly left more than just memories and history. Deeply stained into the very fabric of the capital's folklore, myths and legend are its association with the paranormal. In London, you are too never far away from a ghost.

The capital's theatre industry is almost as old as the city itself. With its foundations rooted firmly in Elizabethan times, the actor has never looked back. During the past 100 years, theatre has grown from strength to strength causing the West End or theatre-land district to become a successful tourist trap and a multi-million pound industry.

Over the past 300 years, millions of theatrical characters have worked beneath the buildings' scenery and chandeliers. It was a way of life for some and an escape from life for others. Throughout this time, those personalities left behind spectral stains in the fabric of the buildings. Superstition is just as common amongst theatre employees today as it was in Shakespeare's time.

With over fifty theatres within the parish of the West End, it comes as no surprise to find out that many of them are said to be supernatural residential homes. Theatrical ghosts are almost as traditional as the smell of the greasepaint and roar of the crowd. In fact, some of them have become spectral celebrities in their own right. The fame that enveloped them on the earth plane has magnified threefold since they passed over.

Ghosts have played a great part in the history of theatre. There has always been a strange relationship between the paranormal and the stage. Shakespeare himself taunted many of his characters with ghosts and ghouls. Many playwrights have followed in the Bard's fondness of apparitions and phenomena; it is certainly a great way to introduce fear and panic. A successful pattern emerged and even today it seems the paranormal certainly appeals to the audience's curiosity of the supernatural.

In the age of the modern musical, ghosts are far from excluded. Andrew Lloyd Webber's *Phantom of the Opera* and *The Woman in White* uses theatrical trickery to entice the audience into belief. In *Miss Saigon*, the ghost of murdered Tui returns to haunt Kim in her dreams, and in *Les Misérables* the entire cast, whose characters have been killed in the revolution, appear once more to sing in joyous harmony.

Our imagination holds no bounds: there are no restrictions, no dead ends, just pure endless thought and creation. In the world of theatre anything is possible and in the space of three hours your adventure is endless. Theatre blends reality and make-believe as its edges are blurred in manmade darkness. In a pool of illusion and shrouded in mystery, theatre can change a scene in a flick of a light. The intensity felt within the industry can be phenomenal – the passion, the hunger, the desperation, the loneliness, the sadness, the elation and the needy. It attracts many of life's misfits and ever-expanding egos. This extreme emotion stains the air and resonates around the building, even when the audience are long gone. Voices echo down the dark corridors soaking into the fabric of the building. A theatre after the show, or first thing in the morning, resembles a playground at night – desolate yet hauntingly alive. Whispers and footsteps play havoc with your hearing, shadows slip and slide into corners and crevices. In the theatre you are never alone. Combine all this with superstition, a vivid imagination, residual emotion, factual validations and psychic information and you have a classic haunting.

The Lyceum Theatre

A Brief History

In 1631, looming tenements and ageing courtyards were built on the site of the future Lyceum Theatre. The crumbling walls constantly blocked out the washed-out sun, spreading eternal damp and moss across the muddy yards. In the shadows, life's darker spices lurked with intent. Within years, the area was home to prostitution, the homeless and scavengers.

In 1765, on the nearby grounds of Exeter House, an exhibition and concert hall was built. Called 'The Lyceum,' it was the first of six theatre-style buildings that hovered on and around the present site. In 1834 (situated slightly west of today's building) the theatre was renamed the Royal Lyceum and English Opera House. By the late nineteenth century, the surrounding area was, by night, a haven for brothels and debauchery, yet the theatres remained the jewels in the dirt and grime.

In 1878 theatrical history was about to be made, when actor manager Sir Henry Irving took over the lease. Henry was the first actor manager to be knighted, and became one of the leading lights of that century. Another name, not normally associated with theatre, is Bram Stoker. Bram worked at the Lyceum as business manager for Sir Henry Irving for twenty years, whilst executing his passion to write. *Dracula* was supposedly written during this time, and it is said that Irving's mannerisms were the inspiration for the Count, so much so that Stoker wanted Irving to play the part in a stage version. In 1898 the theatre was witness to a massive fire in the scene dock. By 1904 the Lyceum had reached yet another crevice in its expansive history and was forced to close due to financial problems. The new owners rebuilt it yet again and managed to drive its success on for another thirty years, but by 1939 the site was destined to be demolished and resurrected as a traffic roundabout in a new road system. However, the Second World War brought chaos to future town planning. During the dark years of war the theatre remained derelict and closed.

In 1945 the theatre was brought by Mecca and opened as dance hall. In the late 1980s the theatre was closed and boarded up. In 1996, the Lyceum opened with the revival of *Jesus Christ Superstar.* In 1999 Disney's *Lion King* roared loudly with a successful run.

The Lyceum Theatre Interviews

One of the most famous ghost stories attached to the Lyceum is over 150 years old. Back in the late 1800s, a couple of wealthy gentry were watching an opera from one of the boxes. The man, whose name has been lost in time, looked down into the stalls and was shocked to see the

The Lyceum Theatre.

severed head of a cavalier, sitting in the lap of a lady watching the performance. The eyes were pointing straight at him, cold and dark. The man was frightened, yet waited until the interval before he went down into the auditorium to investigate further. The lady was gone and so was the head, leaving the man perplexed. It was not until several years later, when the man was visiting friends in Yorkshire, that he noticed an old painting hanging on the wall. To his surprise it was the face of the cavalier; his friend informed him the portrait was of Henry Courtenay who was beheaded during the Civil War. It was rumoured that back in the seventeenth century, Henry's family also owned the land upon which the Lyceum is now built. On the other hand, the ghost was also rumoured to be the spectral figure of Madame Tussaud, complete with waxwork head, for she held her first ever exhibition there back in the early nineteenth century. The head was never seen again and the mystery remains unsolved.

There were many reports of a man-like corpse walking the corridors of the theatre, but it completely disappeared in 1945, when the theatre was used as a dance hall. Recently, the paranormal activity has been prevalent. The theatre is said to be haunted by several entities: the frequently seen lady in grey, a lonely middle-aged man and a threatening invisible presence. Annette Hannigan, assistant FOH manger, explains, 'A previous manager was walking down towards the Grand Circle, when suddenly, a man walked out of a wall , tipped his hat, and said good morning, then, disappeared, it seems the Grand Circle is a hive of activity'. Rachel Cantrill, who also works front of house, agrees, 'When I walk away from the Grand and towards the Irving Suite, I always feel a presence behind me; it has happened so many times, something is up. I class myself as a believer, but I don't know what this powerful feeling is'.

There have been countless reports from ushers, of strange presences following them down certain corridors. Annette Hannigan continues:

Another previous manager followed a lady down one of the corridors, no-one was in the building. The lady, dressed in a grey cloak, ignored the mangers calls and walked into a wall. It is said, this particular female spirit was Mrs Irving, walking around her long gone flat, it is rumoured that the flat used to be in the vicinity of the Grand Circle ... Apparently, Sir Henry Irving was a brandy drinking alcoholic and he had a habit of knocking over brandy glasses to stop himself drinking it. When ever a Brandy glass is placed on the side bar, today, it goes flying off, hence we no longer have Brandy glasses anywhere in the theatre.

Peter Rowalik has been the cleaning supervisor for five years. Early one morning, he was checking the Royal Circle toilets when all of a sudden the door swung open and a lady in a bonnet and long grey coat walked in. She entered one of the cubicles and then disappeared. Peter was dumbstruck and promptly left. He reported the intruder to the security, who informed him the building was empty.

The apparitions are only one type of haunting in the theatre; the other type is a little more menacing. It first started in the Royal Circle bar, as spirit rapping, obscure tapping from within the walls and inside cupboards. This developed into very loud bangs, then there were many reports of ushers being pushed in the Stalls toilets as the activity has progressed violently. In the Grand Circle toilets, all the doors to the cubicles started banging at once. This paranormal phenomenon has been witnessed by the staff and by members of the audience.

Sara Runesson, who works front of house, has probably had the most frightening experience to date. It happened during the show when Sara was in the cellar. She had put some bottles away in a cupboard and was closing the door, when all of a sudden the door pushed itself back open. So strong was the force it knocked her over. Sara screamed and ran from the cellar. On the way she reported it to a colleague, who just pushed it aside. Sara was terrified, then, as if to prove a point, a thunderous rumble and bang echoed from the cellar. Both their jaws dropped but bravely they went to find out what caused this uproar. The cellar was silent and still, nothing had moved and the cupboard door was closed.

The Lyceum Investigation

Location: The top window/site of Bram Stoker's office
Reported activity: None
Investigation: Becky felt the stairs were not part of the present building, more like part of another room. Becky said, 'I am picking up a presence that comes across as a complete neurotic or an absolute mental genius. I feel they were on the verge of borderline madness and that they were using opium, because I feel the high and low energy wasn't their own thoughts. I can see the tearing of pages, as if someone is judgmental of their work'. *Fact: it was confirmed this area used to be an office that belonged to Bram Stoker (rumour has it that Bram wrote* Dracula *from this office).*

Location: Upper Circle Corridor
Reported activity: Apparitions of a grey lady
Investigation: A woman was picked upon who looked just like a Jane Austin character, but she presents herself carrying a flower, which means remembrance. She had something to do with the theatre. *Fact: there are two ladies primarily associated with the building's past – could the grey lady be the ghost of Ellen Terry or Madame Tussaud?*

Location: Auditorium/ Upper Circle
Reported activity: Apparitions of a lady
Investigation: Becky picked up on animals in a circus. She knew that the show was *The Lion King* and that there were a lot of animal costumes and puppets onstage, but Ian saw real animals on stage; he saw a circus. *Fact: There was a circus that performed here on the stage nearly 300 years ago.*

Location: The Upper Circle Bar
Reported activity: Odd feelings, uncomfortable presences
Investigation: A sweeping energy is discovered, which pulls the team together making them feel very nauseous. 'This is an energy vortex, or possibly a port hole, a doorway', claimed Becky. 'It's a link between this world and another world, a doorway between two worlds. It's like a worm hole in space, where two energy systems meet. Spirit uses it to pop in and out of dimensions'. But why is it there? Becky felt it would make sense if someone had been holding some kind of ritual or ceremony, for example, if they dabbled with things like magic or witchcraft and did not realise what they were doing.

Becky felt opium was used to help them write, 'It is well known that drugs can damage your aura and open holes that could attract a negative energy'. Due to the subject matter of *Dracula* Ian and Becky both felt Bram Stoker became obsessed with something dark. It is confirmed that Mary Shelly, Bram Stoker, and Lord Byron used to take opium. Was it used to encourage the imagination in order to create their Gothic tales? *Fact: Ian later discovered that the abuse of opium during the last century was rife in all classes, although it was very popular with the upper classes.*

Location: The Royal Circle (Crush) Bar
Reported activity: Spirit rapping
Investigation: *Fact: The bar is alleged to be the original dining room of Sir Henry Irving.* Becky felt drained and suggested the vortex may pull energy from this room. Calling out, the group took it in turns to ask, 'Is there anybody there? Would you like to talk to us? Please make a noise'. After each question there was a silent pause. All of a sudden a massive bang was heard in the corner. The sound came from within the building, within the room. They all jumped. They asked the ghost to repeat the sound. Nothing was heard. Was this paranormal? There are certainly no explanations to how or why the bang was made. Once again, the silence returned.

Location: The cellar
Reported activity: Violent poltergeist activity and auditory phenomena
Investigation: Becky felt she had found the root of the vortex that runs throughout the building; there was an immense pressure of energy emanating from one of cupboard doors. Many of the ushers will not come down here alone.

Conclusion   Haunted Scale: 8-10
Ian – Ghosts are the one thing I would expect to see in this particular theatre. Its theatrical history is traced as far back as the seventeenth century, so it came as no surprise to find the theatre has countless spooks. However, I feel the majority of ghost sightings are explainable. In order to look at the supernatural, we have to eradicate the natural. I feel that 95 per cent of all sightings are a mixture of imagination, natural phenomena, psychic energy and the power of suggestion. The last 5 per cent is the result of a residual replay of time and emotion. The residual imprint is still incredibly paranormal as we can only suggest how and why this can occur. I feel a vast majority of the sightings at the Lyceum are the result of this type of phenomena.

The identity of the Grey Lady remains unknown, although the staff have named her Mrs Irving. It was interesting to discover that it was documented that Henry Irving was married but in the early years of his life. However, the ghost of the Grey Lady could possibly be the actress Ellen Terry (who worked alongside Irving). In the box office, there is an old photograph of Ellen which looks uncannily similar to the apparition that has been regularly seen.

Slamming doors and falling glasses are all typical examples of poltergeist activity. What causes this? There are several possibilities which range from angry grounded spirits to highly charged psychic energy which is expelled from us or from nature. This energy is usually centred on a person who is referred to as an agent or focus. It would be interesting to find out whether this type of activity is commonplace around the few employees who have experienced it.

The vortex of energy is definitely apparent in several of the rooms front of house. Is this the outcome of some sort of electrical spill or has it actually been conjured up by someone. I feel this is probably a by-product of a natural phenomenon. There is definitely energy present and whatever the explanation, you will not be able to stand in it for long before feeling nauseous.

Becky – It could be my love of vampires that first made the connection with Bram Stocker so exiting. I have never come across an energy vortex as large at the one at the Lyceum. In my work, I believe in dispelling fear, as fear can encourage the problem further. I was worried about enhancing the employee's fears by writing this story and bringing it to a head, however it is a fact of life that there are as many positives as there are negatives. Universal law says like attracts like, therefore all the good people that work in the building will be safe if they live without fear in their hearts. I feel no one working at this theatre has anything to fear from the vortex.

The Adelphi Theatre

Previously founded as Sans Pareli in 1806, this present building is the fourth to be built. In 1897 the actor William Terriss was murdered outside the stage door by fellow actor Richard Prince. William was one of the country's most popular actors of the period and his murder caused a media storm. It seems Richard Prince became infatuated with William's success and thought his fame hampered his own celebrity. Prince was reported to say, 'I did it for revenge. He had kept me out of employment for ten years, and I had either to die in the street or kill him'. William's ghost is rumoured to have haunted the building ever since and his apparition has been seen both inside and outside the theatre. (Surprisingly, his ghost is also rumoured to haunt Covent Garden tube station.) Could he be responsible for reported poltergeist phenomena? This haunting could be the result of residual energy left over from the murder of Terriss.

The emotional stain of murder is said to stay in the ether for eons. Is this visual phenomenon just a bookmark in time replaying the horrific event? One fact is certain – the residual ghost is non-interactive. Even though he was killed, the spirit of William Terriss would have passed successfully over to the spirit world leaving behind a double image or stain. During the recent run of *Chicago*, an electrician was working onstage late one night, when suddenly he turned around to see an auditorium full of people. But spookily, the image was slightly out of kilter. It appeared the audience were not sitting in the modern seating. Once again we could apply the release of residual energy as a reasonable explanation to this strange sight. But what causes the overlap of imagery? One theory could be that the electrician's mind could add the pictures to the frame and just fill in the gaps, or did he actually see the ghosts of an old audience?

The Adelphi Theatre

The Dominion Theatre

A Brief History

The Dominion Theatre, Tottenham Court Road, has been one of the capital's leading theatres for the past seventy-six years. In its long and colourful past, it has been the home of many musicals, rock shows and film showings.

The area of St Giles (upon which the theatre is built) was originally marshland and in 1101 AD it was associated with lepers. At this time, Queen Matilda, wife of Henry I, founded a hospital for sufferers of the disease on the site of the future theatre. In 1764, a brewery was built on the site which contained the 'world's biggest porter vat'. The vat stood 22ft high and contained enough beer to supply 1 million people. Unfortunately in 1811, the vat exploded, sending 600,000 gallons of beer flooding out into the dilapidated tenements that surrounded the area. Some buildings collapsed under the strain. Even though it was seen as a massive disaster, it was reported that only eight people died, by either drowning in beer or from being poisoned from the fumes.

In 1911, the Court Cinema opened on the front part of the plot (presently the theatre foyer) and what was left of the brewery (presently the auditorium and backstage area) continued to trade at the back until it was eventually demolished eleven years later. The plot was cleared and a temporary funfair took residence for a while, before it expanded, in 1925, to form 'Luna Park'. The Court Cinema closed in 1928 to make way for the building of a new theatre. The Dominion Theatre as we know it today was completed in 1929. From the 1970s to the 1990s,

The Dominion Theatre

many musicals, rock shows, film screenings and one-nighters took place under her Deco chandeliers. The Dominion became one of London's major performance venues.

The Dominion Interviews

Dave Allan has been one of the Dominion's stage doormen for many years. Dave was a sceptic, until one morning he experienced something strange. Part of Dave's job is to unlock the doors that separate the auditorium and foyer. It was early one morning, and Dave was standing at the back of the auditorium and looking at the stage. He noticed what seemed to be a man standing in front of the safety curtain. The stranger was dressed in a leather apron and appeared to be hitting a stopper into a beer barrel. Although he could hear the banging, the man seemed to be totally oblivious to Dave. He recalls that the strangest thing was, he could only see the figure from the waist up! Dave has now seen this apparition over twenty times. Very occasionally, whilst locking up the dressing rooms at the end of the night, Dave has heard strange banging echoing around the stairwells and corridors. He is alone and the last person out. The building is empty!

J.P. James was the other stage doorman. He, too, witnessed something whilst locking up. The event took place when the theatre was 'dark'. Out of the blue, J.P. heard the sound of heavy footsteps from a nearby stairwell. J.P. double-checked that everyone had gone home. They had. This time he decided to walk around the corridors. He then heard what can be only described as, a child laughing and giggling. Upon reaching the second-floor corridor, he witnessed a fire door open and close on its own. It looked as if someone or something had walked through them. There was no draft.

The second-floor corridor has been the setting for other paranormal activity. The show in residence was *Grease* and the location was dressing room 27. Danny Twoomy, who was the resident house electrician, recalls, 'One of the female cast had been in the room when suddenly she was blatantly hit in the face by a light bulb'. The bulb was checked by the electric department. No explanation could be found. Unfortunately this happened again, a short time later.

Danny himself has had a strange experience in dressing room 27. He was just completing a routine job when he went to open the door but it would not open. He had the key, therefore it was impossible to lock from the other side, but the strangest thing of all is that he heard a child singing down the corridor. Whilst editing this book, we have been told an actor on the current show has seen a Victorian girl in this particular corridor.

Kerstin Muller, deputy master carpenter on *We Will Rock You* betters the previous stories, 'Very occasionally, round the stairwell close to dressing room 27 and out of the corner of my eye, I have seen what looks like a mist hovering around shoulder height. The mist is no larger than a football and white in colour'.

Another area which Kerstin thinks has paranormal interest is under the stage and the former orchestra pit (now home to the hydraulic tube-station truck and series of traps used on *We will Rock You*) the area has a definite air about it, some say spooky.

One afternoon Kerstin was walking up the stage-right staircase to the stage level when she heard someone walking behind her. She turned around to say hello, but to her amazement no one was there. So she carried on, and so did the footsteps. This has apparently happened on a number of occasions. Also, there are reports of employees who have tried to open doors to the sub-stage, only to feel as if there is someone pushing them shut. The other active area under the stage is the orchestra pit. Kerstin, who operates the hydraulics, often gets that feeling she is not alone. Sometimes the experience is so frightening that she has to leave to room.

Alex Sayer had been working as backstage crew for a few weeks when she saw something she could not explain. Sitting alone at the back of the hydraulic cage, she saw a shadowy black figure. The apparition, who she believes to be a man, walked through one of the caged doors. The door was closed. The alleged spectre walked a few feet then disappeared.

'During the run of *Grease*, a couple of employees decided to play around with a Ouija board after the show one night', says Andy Sutherland the resident fireman. They reported that several entities were supposedly contacted. One was particularly aggressive, one died in the former leper hospital and the other was sitting in the auditorium watching the debacle on stage. They also managed to contact the spirit of an unfortunate stagehand who had overdosed.

There have been countless reports of people sensing a presence behind them and stories of a woman or a black shadow. The current show is the queen musical *We Will Rock You* and it comes as no surprise to discover that the ghost of Freddie Mercury has been seen. Ian says, 'I worked on the Queen musical and have seen, what I believe to be the energy of Freddie. It was during 'We are the Champions' I had felt a presence behind me whilst I was cueing the show, then I clairvoyantly saw him watching the show from the wings and criticising it'. Becky also worked for a short while on the show. She, too, alongside other cast members, has felt energy. Jenna Lee James felt Freddie moved through her as she sung one of his ballads.

The Dominion Investigation

Location: Second-floor Corridor and Dressing Room 27
Reported activity: White mist, auditory poltergeist phenomena
Investigation: Becky felt very unbalanced, a certain melancholy feeling and slight annoyance. She felt the energy of an old night watchman who used to shuffle around the area. In dressing room 27, she sensed the sad energy of an understudy. A light anomaly was captured in the corridor.

Location: Sub-stage and the orchestra pit
Reported activity: An apparition of a cloaked man, moving shadows, foreboding atmospheres, colds spots and general poltergeist activity
Investigation: Becky and Ian felt nauseous. Becky felt someone drowned in chemicals and could sense a terrible smell. She said, 'I get the impression like there was an unexpected gush of water that pushed forward'. *Fact: In 1811, the world's biggest beer vat exploded, sending a wave of beer out into the street killing several people.*

Becky grabbed her arm in pain, 'I've got the impression of pain in my arm and a limp, I feel like I'm in a hospital but not allowed out. I sense it's like a quarantine area and I'm waiting to die'. *Fact: In the twelfth century, the area was known to house a leper hospital. Could the pain and limp be associated with leprosy?*

Location: The upper circle, auditorium
Reported activity: Strange moving shadows, the apparition of a Victorian lady
Investigation: Both Becky and Ian felt the energy of an old man. He showed himself sitting in one of the seats. They felt he passed over successfully with throat cancer. The ghost of the man loves the theatre and visits it regularly.

Conclusion   Haunted Scale: 7 -10
Ian – The land upon which the Dominion stands has witnessed some negative events throughout the past 800 years. Even today, the area feels oppressive and attracts life's flotsam and jetsam. The reported paranormal activity is mostly residual energy interlaced with classic poltergeist phenomena. Most poltergeist activity centres around a focus or agent, therefore we must look into who occupied dressing room 27 in the past. It is usually associated with emotional turmoil and angst which explodes externally as psychic energy. This type of phenomena is sometimes referred to as 'telekinesis – the ability of the mind to influence matter or energy'. The sub-stage area and orchestra pit is probably at the medieval ground level, therefore the foreboding feelings and moving shadows could be the residual replay of past events. The young girl and sounds of children playing only present themselves in the corridors backstage. This could be the level of the Court Cinema which was built in 1911 and would explain the period clothing the girl was wearing. I believe this to be purely residual. Once again the theatre is haunted but only by memory, however I feel the presence of Freddie Mercury is felt and his image witnessed, but manifested by thought and intention.

Becky – I am convinced that the theatre has its ghosts, although they come in visitation. I believe many spirits come to the theatre to enjoy the energy of the show. During our investigation, there was no evidential proof that the theatre was haunted as such, although the story about the actress who had a bulb thrown at her was very interesting. The strongest energy seems to centre on the sub-stage area, and I have seen shadows moving out of the corner of my eye.

The Novello Theatre

Built in 1905, The Novello was originally called the Strand Theatre. A mischievous ghost is said to be responsible for moving costumes, wigs and props in this Edwardian theatre. Recently, a staff member stayed the night in one of the bars and awoke as an entrancing eerie feeling overcame her. Fear can play havoc on our conscious mind and cause further hampering to our subconscious

The Novello Theatre

mind. Staying overnight in an old building will tease the imagination to some extent. Most of us are scared of the unknown, a feeling that can be traced back to a primeval flight or fight reaction. Look what would happen if a domestic cat was put in an alien environment: it would immediately become frightened and cautious and jump at the slightest noise. Why should we be any different? Why would a ghost want to move costumes and wigs? It could be the result of an overzealous cleaner. On the other hand, it could be the result of extreme poltergeist behaviour.

The London Palladium

A Brief History

In 1571, the site of the Palladium consisted of meadows and muddy pathways and on the horizon the Elizabethan city of London huddled together its rooftops. In 1737, the Duke of Argyll acquired the land and built his London home. Argyll House was built in traditional eighteenth-century style over a bowling green and summer house. It was a typical Georgian town house, although it was said to be quite plain. On either side of the house a carpenter and a bricklayer plied their trades. The site has been used for a multitude of different purposes. It has been a vaulted wine cellar, the 'Old Pantheon Bazaar', the 'Corinthian Bazaar and exhibition rooms', an indoor circus, and the National Skating Palace.

In 1909, it was decided the land was to be completely altered in order to build a music hall. In 1910, the Variety Theatre opened and the rest, they say, is history. After ninety-five years of entertainment, it is said, if you topped the bill at the Palladium, you were a star. The Palladium became, and still is, one of the West End's most famous theatres.

The London Palladium Interviews

It is recorded that the Palladium is haunted by the Crimson Lady. She has been seen many times gliding up and down the Old Crimson Staircase at the back of the Royal Circle. It is suggested she could be one of two women, Lady Helen Campbell, who was a former resident of Argyle House, or possibly Mrs Shireburn, the mistress of the Duke of Argyle.

Linford, has been working at the Palladium since 1963, says, 'There's ghosts all over this place'. Part of his job as an LX charge hand is to turn all the lights off at night. It was during this time that he saw a lady by the Royal Circle, standing and looking towards the stage. There was no interaction. The lady looked very Victorian in dress. Could this be the ghost of the Crimson Lady?

The spot box is situated at the very back of the auditorium. Linford recalls, 'This place is very strange, Doors open and close on there own and often you can feel a presence beside you, then I feel I feel like I'm burning up'. Backstage, there is a corridor called 'The Elephant Run' (an area used in pantomimes to allow access for live animals) and this has been a location where strange things have been seen. It is an area of the theatre that has been forgotten about for decades and like a time capsule to the theatre world of the 1950s, it remains hidden from the twenty-first century by an insignificant door. Like a secret room, the old stairwells and wardrobe department are condemned, but represent a perfect setting for a haunting. A more gruesome fact is confirmed under the stage. The ashes of two people are interred in a wall. Could this be the cause of the strange activity?

The Palladium

The Palladium Investigation
Location: The whole building
Reported activity: Sightings of a crimson lady, general poltergeist activity, presences
Investigation: Becky senses the energy of a geeky looking comedian; another team member feels as if there is a slight negative energy is associated with him. Moving towards the stage, Becky surprisingly feels the residual energy of famous medium, Doris Stokes, 'I felt she had a bandage on her left leg, which was covered by a long dress. I get the feeling she is saying that she can see every single face of the audience. I think she would swear sometimes to. That sweet little old lady comes across a very strong-willed character'.

Conclusion   Haunted Scale: 1 -10
Ian – I was convinced we would come across some verifiable validations associated with the alleged haunting of the Palladium but the building was not going to give up its secrets. With so many large egos and personalities within the theatre's history, I thought the residual imprints would be waiting to greet us. Doris Stokes did play to packed houses at the theatre, but that is a well-known fact. I felt her energy was only a faint residue. I was very interested in the legend of the Crimson Lady and her residual haunting. However, if she is an alleged past resident of the ancient Argyle House, why is she seen standing on a fairly modern staircase built for the theatre? I feel the apparition is probably a character from a much later period; it is suggested that the lady could even be a member of royalty.

Becky – I expected to step out onto the stage at the Palladium and really feel something special. It's one of the most famous venues in London and one that is renowned for having the most famous people and mediums perform there. My only guess is that many of the mediums have performed a form of spirit release or space clearing as I found it hard even to feel any atmosphere at all – truly not what I was expecting.

The Phoenix Theatre

A Brief History
The Phoenix Theatre has existed for seventy-five years. Slipped rather uncomfortably between a secondhand bookshop and a guitar shop on Charing Cross Road, you may never see her. The only recognisable sign that you are passing a theatre is the fading patchwork of cast photographs representing over fourteen years of performances of the musical *Blood Brothers*.

The theatre, built in 1930, is situated on the site of the west boundary wall of the old medieval hospital of St Giles. The parish of St Giles was always a very unruly place and in the seventeenth century it has decayed into a cut-throat, cloak-and-daggered slum. The many tenements became overcrowded, and were infamous, polluted dens of antiquity. For the next 200 years, life's misfits, gamblers, prostitutes and gangsters curdled their way through the cess pits. It was not until the big clean up during the late nineteenth century that the area begin to breathe again and things start to improve. It was reported that the slums of St Giles were the most squalid in London at that time.

Charing Cross Road was built in 1877 and etched its way north through the newly sculpted St Giles, a new trend into the area. Built on the back of the early twentieth-century buildings which fronted Charing Cross Road was a music hall rather exotically named the Alcazar. The Alcazar was unlicensed and well known for its 'dodgy, moral character'. It was home to the sleazy underdog, attractive to rogues and ladies of the night. Today, the Alcazar lives on, but only in the name of the modern block of flats grafted onto the back of the theatre.

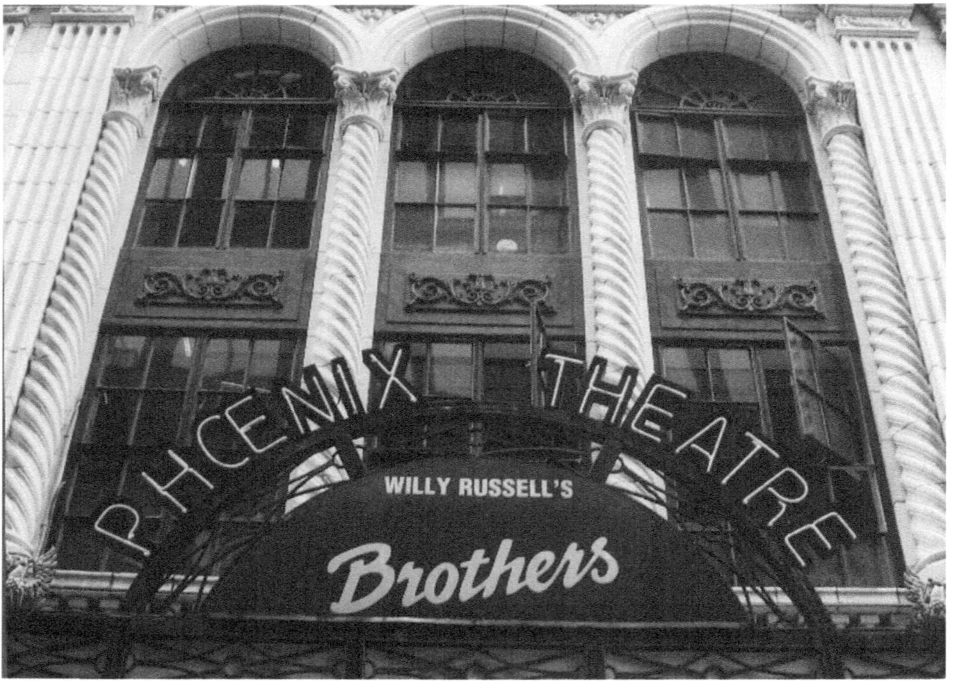

The Phoenix Theatre

The Phoenix Interviews

Richard Kingcott is deputy stage manager on *Blood Brothers* and is keen to explain his paranormal encounters:

> Unfortunately, a number of years ago, Stephanie Laurence, who played Mrs Johnson, died. It was a tremendous shock and she was, and still is, dearly missed. One day during the show, I was sitting in prompt corner, when I saw Stephanie dressed as Mrs Johnson standing in one of the doorways of the set on the other side of the stage. I didn't think any thing of it, until I suddenly realised, Stephanie had died twelve years ago.

Lisa Tempest has seen a white light gliding along the backstage passage from stage right to stage left. She feels that this was the spirit of Stephanie Lawrence, as this was the area of the set associated with Stephanie's character. This is also the area that Becky encountered an energy which appeared to walk straight through her. 'When I was working at the Phoenix, I felt many presences at the theatre. On one occasion, as I walked behind the set, I suddenly stepped right into one or it maybe it stepped through me'.

Richard has had many unexplainable experiences in the theatre. He has felt the presence of Stephanie several times since the apparition. But Stephanie's energy is not the only energy he has sensed backstage. During one particular part of the show, and only when the character Eddie is onstage, Richard feels someone standing behind him. It is rumoured to be the ghost of one of original actors that played Eddie who unfortunately died a number of years previously. Becky also sensed something similar, 'Whist I was learning to cue the show, I felt a presence standing behind me, only to turn and see no one there'.

Daniel Carter is box-office manager. He recalls a more foreboding feeling in the theatre. The mirrored corridor that runs along the back of the auditorium has a strange air about it. He says that the FOH staff do not like walking down it. Could it be the supposed ghost of an old theatre manager who has been seen at the back of the auditorium?

The Phoenix Investigation

Location: The mirrored corridor, front of house

Reported activity: Un-nerving feelings, sightings of an old theatre manager

Investigation: Becky immediately sensed a matronly type of woman. 'She presents herself to me wearing a grey pinafore dress and white blouse. Her lips are pursed and I have the sense she has a large chest'. Becky sensed that the matron sees the corridor as her own space which she patrols. 'I feel she is only residual energy, because I sense her as a see-through image rather than being a vibration or solid matter'.

Location: The stage left wing and onstage

Reported activity: Light anomalies, apparition of Stephanie Laurence, unusual presences in prompt corner.

Investigation: Walking across the set, Becky picked up a female energy, 'I feel she has really big eyes; she is a really beautiful lady, but very concerned about her weight and a little kind of chubby. I feel you may often see her crossing the stage and going through that door. I can just feel her residual energy here, but I don't think she is here today, I feel she only comes and visits every so often'. They stopped by prompt corner, 'When I worked here, I was very aware of a presence behind me. I finally realised there was a pattern emerging; the presence only appeared during Eddie's scenes. It felt stronger when there was an understudy on. I tuned into him and I gave a complete description of what he looked like to the company manager, who looked shocked and then named him. This unfortunate actor died young. *Blood Brothers* was his last job. It meant a lot to him, so I felt he visits just to check on the new cast'.

Conclusion   Haunted Scale: 5 -10

Ian – I was convinced the Phoenix was going to be a theatre riddled with ghosts. I had heard so many stories about the unfortunate Stephanie Laurence; she had a sad end to her life but she loved the show. I feel that the spirit of Stephanie has passed successfully over into the spirit world, but an essence of her will always remain. Mix in the residual replay and we have her ghost. I feel this can explain the apparitions. Since Stephanie's death, stories of her ghost sightings may have injected the residual with thought, creating a visual image which has been manifested by the living. A similar situation has occurred with the alleged ghost of Eddie. Does his spirit appear in visitation, checking out his competition? It's a nice thought but I personally feel any physical feelings attached to the actor's life are shed when they pass over. We are only picking up the emotion left behind, but sometimes that feeling is so strong we sense it is associated with spirit. Nevertheless, all these feelings and apparitions are classic examples of a haunting,

Becky – One of the things that I discovered whilst working on this show is, because of the sad ending, it can leave a negative feeling. It is a fantastic show, but the energy left can imprint into the fabric of the building. Even though I sensed the energy of Stephanie and the actor who played Eddie, this was only residual. However, I did sense that they visit the theatre at times, when their spirit comes from the spirit world to visit friends or to spend time in a place they enjoyed during their lives on this earth.

Noel Coward Theatre

Sir Charles Wyndham was responsible for building the theatre in 1903 and it is rumoured that his ghost walks the dressing-room corridors. Both Becky and Ian have found it incredibly interesting to discover that the majority of ghosts seen around the West End seem to be past theatre managers.

The Fortune Theatre

A Brief History

Dwarfed by her neighbour, the Theatre Royal Drury Lane, the Fortune Theatre is often forgotten, but she has bathed in the shadow of the 'Lane' for longer than most of the West End theatres. In fact it is rumoured that the Fortune Theatre lies on, or nearby, the site of the Elizabethan Cockpit Theatre. The Cockpit, as its name suggests, started life in 1609 as a venue for cock-fighting before it morphed into the Playhouse Theatre, which was immediately burnt down by a rioting mob. It was rebuilt and was suitably renamed The Phoenix as it rose from the ashes. However, in 1665 it was forced to close again owing to the completion of the Theatre Royal.

The Fortune is situated on the edge of London's Covent Garden Market. The area became very popular after the Great Fire of 1666 and flourished into the next century. By the early 1700s the market and its surrounding area was well known for its dubious reputation. Gambling dens and brothels were rife and most homes were turned into seedy lodgings and Turkish baths. The area was renowned for prostitution, yet it also became known for its theatre industry. A century later, the site of the Future Theatre became home to the Albion Tavern, a famous drinking hole for Victorian actors.

Built on Russell Street, in Covent Garden in 1924, the Fortune was the first theatre to be erected after the First World War. The building had a chequered history as productions go and this lasted nearly sixty years. It was not until 1989 when the present show at the time of writing, *The Woman in Black*, opened did things look up. The show has been very successful and one of the longest running in the West End.

The Fortune Interviews

The Fortune's morning stage-door keeper is Amanda Sim. She recounts a few haunting tales about the theatre and the show. 'There have been sightings of a manifestation. Half shadow, half woman'. One of the main characters in *The Woman in Black* is a ghost who walks around the stage during the play. On one particular performance, a main cast member thought he saw was the actress (who plays the ghost) in the wings – nothing unusual in itself, but it was only when he realised at this particular point of the play that the actress was actually behind him onstage did he get scared. He was very spooked. The apparition of a woman in black has been seen many times. Stranger still is that the apparition is only seen during summertime.

Natalie Block plays the ghost of the woman, but even she has seen her spectral mirror image. Natalie has been playing the ghost for six years, but her connection to the play and the theatre goes back many years. She first worked in the theatre as an usher and it was then that she first saw the ghost:

The Fortune Theatre

I was sitting at the back of the dress circle during a performance, when I noticed a grey shadow in Box A. The shadow took the form of a lady. Rationally and level-headedly, I turned away assuming it to be a trick of the light. To my surprise, when I looked again the lady was still there. I could even make out her clothes. She wore what looked like a turn-of-the-century corseted dress. Her hair was worn up in a Victorian style. The lady sat still watching the show. I turned away again, I couldn't believe my eyes. I looked back again and but the apparition was gone.

The management revelled in the fact that the theatre possibly had a ghost and informed the press which caused a tremendous amount of interest and a story appeared in the national news. A paranormal investigation team was brought in to catch the ghost. Apart from dramatic changes in temperature, an alleged sign of spiritual activity, they found nothing.

Part of Natalie's job as an usher was to spend time in the small hospitality room attached to Box A. This was a little unnerving as the ghost was actually seen in that very box. Natalie felt the room itself had a terrible feeling about it and had quite a foreboding air.

During the show, Natalie has to spend a considerable amount of time in the stage right wing. She noticed that this wing also had an oppressive feeling. It made her nervous and a little scared. She then started smelling perfume, which seemed to follow her around the building. She also said she could smell pipe smoke and whenever she was under the stage she could smell 'sewerage or rotting flesh!'

Whilst performing as the ghost, Natalie had to appear to glide around upstage behind gauze. Suddenly she became aware of an explainable shadow moving in the stage right wing. Natalie described it as 'moving darkness'. In the scene, the ghost (Natalie) had to frighten the young actor, Sebastian, and glide off into the stage right wing with Sebastian following. On this occasion, Sebastian was in a terrible state as he watched Natalie walk offstage and into the outstretched arms of a ghost of a woman in black! At the time, Natalie saw nothing but after the event her skin crawled. The ghost of the woman in black has been seen many times over the years but on further investigation we discovered that she has only been seen since Natalie has been in the building.

The Fortune Investigation

Location: Box A

Reported activity: Apparition of woman dressed in black

Investigation: Becky almost immediately sensed an energy, 'There is something here with us and I can feel it; I think that it's a traditional woman in grey or black that people may have seen'. Has this woman been seen? As she sat in the actual spot where the ghost had been seen, Becky tuned into her energy, 'I have the distinct impression of an elderly lady. She just sits here, although she doesn't watch the show. It's not the show that she's interested in; it's the people, the audience. If I was down there in the stalls I would maybe get a glimpse of her, look back again and she's gone. I feel she thinks she is holding court'. The team heard several unexplained bangs from the back of the stalls. Becky allowed the energy to overshadow her face. All the team members noticed a distinct change in Becky's facial features. The photographer manages to capture the phenomena on film, which spookily resembles the made-up face of Natalie. Becky said, 'She is a very powerful spirit, she is very controlling. She is timeless. She is unaware of time, whether it is today or next week. She is aware of me but it's like I am a ghost in her dimension'.

Location: Stage right wing

Reported activity: Apparition of a woman in black, foreboding feelings, unexplainable smells

Investigation: Becky instantly picked up a man, 'He is someone who barks at people, he is quite strong about it; he had, and still has, an attitude. I wouldn't be surprised if there are two people to do with the show that have crossed over'. Two of the team experienced tinnitus at the same time. Becky and Ian both felt that someone associated with this theatre was involved in a traffic accident. Ian and the photographer witnessed a light anomaly which resembled an outline or thread of gossamer. Becky announced, 'There is someone standing on my right-hand side; they are listening to us and are interested in what we are doing'. We discovered that the energy may be a recent female company manager who was unfortunately killed during a road accident as she travelled to the theatre. It turns out this lady was also a personal friend of our photographer. Sandy the photographer recalls, 'Yes, she was a friend of mine and also killed in a road accident, I remember wanting to get some classical music for her, because she had something wrong her ears, you know, tinnitus'. There was a sudden cold draft that blows across the wing.

Conclusion   Haunted Scale: 8-10

Becky – In Box A, I allowed the energy to get so close to me, I could feel her presence. I gave her permission to overlay her face on mine. The 'woman in black' was not a ghost as one might first expect! This was a prime example of a 'thought form' manifested from energy created by the fear of the audience and the belief of the actors. A thought form cannot exist without energy as it has none of its own. The play has been running for seventeen years and in that time, the 'thought form' has been given enough energy it has come into being. I also feel the spirit has a strong link with Natalie who plays the role of the woman in black. She is very sensitive and has given a lot of belief and energy to the ghost. I had to make a decision. Do I move it on or do I leave it alone. It seems the energy is not doing any harm to anyone. In fact it adds atmosphere to the show and the theatre.

Ian – This investigation was held after the evening performance. Sitting in a dark empty theatre can certainly play with your eyes and mind. The ghost of the woman in black is most definitely not residual; she is also not an aspect of psychic energy. In fact, I also feel she is the result of a 'thought form manifestation'. We completely underestimate the power of the mind. I feel the mind can start to see sense in chaos or add one to one and come up with three. I feel this apparition is an extension of the actor's mind, the image to the emotion, a multi-faceted explanation also teased by the mystery and fear from the supernatural play. I felt we all perceived energy overshadow Becky's face, but was it due to the power of suggestion? It is interesting that Sandy captured a similar image on film, but presently we cannot exclude the fact that the photo was taken with a SLR camera with night portrait mode, which incidentally can cause the blurred overlay effect. I am very excited that both myself and another team member experienced tinnitus, shortly before Becky sensed the company manager who unbeknown to us suffered from this problem. This is also confirmed by Sandy the photographer who actually knew her. The Fortune is definitely a haunted theatre although haunted by the mind's power of manifestation.

The Palace Theatre

Built in 1891 as The Royal English Opera House, the theatre is said to harbour many ghosts. The spectre of ballerina Anna Pavolva is said to have been seen in the theatre on regular occasions. Her image is said to appear protruding halfway out of the stage floor. Another former ballet dancer's ghost is said to be the cause of erratic poltergeist activity in dressing room 12a. The theatre roof is rumoured to be haunted by the ghost of a dog. An old theatre manager used to walk his dog on the roof but one day the dog fell off and perished. The apparition of composer,

The Palace Theatre

Ivor Novello, who died in 1951, has been seen watching the performances from the back of the dress circle and also been in the Royal Box dressed in a scarlet-lined cloak.

Former theatre manger, Charles Morton 1892-1904, is also said to haunt the building. During a recent show, one followspot operator had ghostly hands on her shoulders for forty minutes before her headsets were suddenly ripped off her head. Another ballet dancer is also said to haunt one of the stairwells. The story recalls the sad dancer hanged herself. There is no time frame allotted to this story.

There are many myths that circulate around the West End. The Ghost of Anna Pavolva is one of the most famous ghosts associated with this building. Anna performed regularly at the theatre when it was known as The Palace of Varieties. If the original stage was lower than the modern one, it could explain the half manifested image of Pavlova as her residual ghost still dances at the old stage level. Ivor Novello's ghost may well have been seen at some point in the past but the story travels through time with no evidential proof. We have no idea when this was or who saw it, yet a vast majority of us accept the story as fact.

The Pit Theatre, Barbican

A Brief History

The Barbican was built in the 1970s, although its origins can be traced back 1,000 years to when the Romans established London. The name 'Barbican' comes from the Latin word *Barbecana*, which meant an outpost or a gateway for an outer defence to a city. In November 1348 the Black Death took hold of the city. The capital could not cope with the amount of burials therefore massive pits were dug outside the city walls. These plague pits are located in nearby the Barbican site.

The inhabitants of the Barbican and London dropped like flies once again in 1665 as the Great Plague extinguished thousands of lives. A year later, a fire was spotted in a baker's shop in Pudding Lane. The rest is history. The Great Fire of London took hold and destroyed most of the medieval city. Luckily, the Barbican was extremely fortunate to escape as the furnace stopped short of a few streets.

The Barbican may have missed the Great Fire by the skin of its teeth but unfortunately 250 years later, it suffered a similar fate. Although the Elizabethan and medieval street planning had gone, most of the warehouses and shops were still relatively tight packed. The buildings stood back-to-back and the fire spread very quickly. The great Cripplegate fire started in one of those warehouses, destroying all in its way. During the outbreak of the Second World War, the whole area of the Barbican suffered from continuous bombing and in 1944 a German flying bomb ended it all. The area was left in rubble. It lay derelict for nearly twenty years before being developed into a new residential project. Most interestingly, when builders began laying foundations here, that they discovered the remains of the original Roman outpost.

The Barbican Interviews

A cleaner who shall remain nameless has had a paranormal experience in The Pit Theatre. Early one morning she was convinced she witnessed a ghost. Could this be a plague victim? Lee Tasker, who has been working at the Barbican for some time, revealed that The Pit was allegedly built on a plague pit. Julian the stage doorman has heard the tale of a spirit woman who walks the many backstage corridors. Jo Hall recounts a story about an experience she had whilst chaperoning a child actor on a show at the The Pit Theatre:

I was working for the Royal Shakespeare Company as a chaperone on a show at The Pit. My child was onstage and I was watching him on the monitor backstage when someone pulled my hair. I turned around thinking it was one of the crew but the wing was completely empty. I could definitely feel a presence around me. I just felt it was a child. I felt it was very playful and trying to get attention. It never happened again but that didn't stop me talking to it when I was at work.

The Barbican Investigation

Location: The Pit Theatre

Reported activity: Unexplained apparitions, hair pulling

Investigation: Becky sensed a fire, 'It feels as if there had been a fire here, or people asphyxiated through smoke inhalation something along those lines. Children died in that fire too. They were used as packers in warehouses. I'm also picking up the energy of a caretaker, an old guy who's got a portly build and is wearing a long black coat, who was in charge of the kids. I can't work out where he's from and he's not really talking to me. The fire started in the cotton press. The caretaker wouldn't let the kids out'. After a spirit release, the team noticed a peculiar vibrating shimmer a few seats back.

Fact: The Great Cripple gate fire ravaged the whole area.

The Barbican Centre

Conclusion   Haunted Scale: 2-10

Ian – I felt the Barbican did not have the sense of a haunted building, even though the residual energy ought to have been seeping from the walls. Plague victims, bombs and fires play a huge part in an alleged haunting but somehow, this enormous complex refuses to spit out its past. We have to ask whether rumour and gossip play a big part in enforcing ghost stories around this building. If we were to actually witness a residual haunting or imprint, it would be at that particular century's original ground level as supposed residual ghosts can only walk on their own ground level. Interestingly, the only reported activity is in The Pit Theatre and surrounding corridors. There is a chance this area lies well below the Barbican's modern street level. Therefore the haunting will occur within the said ether. Could the alleged sightings just be images of those lives gone by?

Becky – It found it almost impossible to psychically read the energy of the building because it is made out of concrete. It is shown that concrete does not withhold the energy as long, for example if you were to leave a car battery on a concrete floor, instead of a brick one, the power would drain out of it quicker. So, any energy absorbed within the walls of the Barbican would have already been transformed or drained. I received the information about the fire and children from my guides.

The Theatre Royal Drury Lane

The Lane is the fourth theatre to be built on this location and probably the most documented haunted theatre in the world. It was built in 1663 which makes it London's oldest theatre. It comes as no surprise to discover the theatre has several infamous ghosts. The Man in Grey usually appears in the guise of an eighteenth-century noble man, with powdered wig, tricorne hat, a dress jacket and cloak, riding boots and a sword. His ghost has been seen in the Upper Circle of the Auditorium. The Man in Grey is said to be the ghost of a murdered man whose skeletal remains, complete with knife stuck in the ribcage, were found within a bricked-up wall. Amazingly, this nameless phantom has been seen by a whole cast who witnessed his appearance during one rehearsal. Legend has it, that 'The Man in Grey's' apparition is a good omen and a sure sign a new show will run.

Comedian and panto dame, Dan Leno (1861-1904) is also said to haunt the theatre. His presence has been sensed in the wings and also noted by the smell of lavender. In 1735, Thomas Hallam was accidentally killed by fellow actor, Charles Macklin, when he thrusted his cane through Hallam's eye during an argument, but it is Charles Macklin's ghost that has been seen wandering the corridors backstage. Clown Joseph Grimaldi (1778-1837) is said to be one of the theatre's most famous ghosts. His spectral foot is allegedly responsible for many phantom kicks received by countless employees but he also guides nervous actors around the stage. West End rumour recalls the story that Grimaldi's face is to appear in the mirror of dressing room 1.

During the run of *Miss Saigon*, a former fireman witnessed a man dressed in 1920s attire walk out of one wall, acknowledge him and then disappear into the opposite wall. Sam Hiller was one of the cast members of *Miss Saigon*. He recounts a strange experience during the start of Act II. Sam witnessed the figure of a woman who appeared to be floating across the seating in the dress circle. He also reported that many of the cast in that scene also saw the phantom lady. Who was she? It is believed to be the ghost of a woman who committed suicide.

Theatre Royal, Drury Lane

The Shaftesbury Theatre

A Brief History

The Shaftesbury Theatre is situated on one of London's oldest thoroughfares. The road was lined with tavern after tavern, some of them notorious for trouble; some of them welcomed a classier traveller. The Maidenhead Inn was a great example and stood a stone's throw from the theatre's site. Once a reputable drinking house, the inn soon declined rapidly into decay and became infamous for beggars, revolting filth and wretchedness. On the site of the stage door, the Vine Tavern was named after the vineyard which occupied the area in the Middle Ages. It seems the area had become associated with many breweries, distilleries and public houses over the centuries. Originally known as the Princes Theatre, it opened on Boxing Day 1911. It was the last theatre to be built on Shaftesbury Avenue. In 1963 it changed its name to The Shaftesbury.

The Shaftesbury Theatre Investigation

Location: Front of House
Reported activity: None
Investigation: Becky said, 'I felt like there was something pushing my stomach, like a winded feeling. It felt like someone had come around the corner too fast and smacked me in the

The Shaftesbury Theatre

stomach with a tray'. Stopping the walk at one of the front-of-house stairwells Becky senses an energy, 'My guide has shown me a man with keys going down the stairs. He really struggles. I feel this guy really had trouble breathing and used to smoke. I also think he used to sleep in the building at night'. *Fact: The theatre used to have a permanent fireman who would stay overnight and carry chains, although there is no record of him dying.*

Conclusion   Haunted Scale: 0–10
Ian – This was our first theatre with no alleged recorded phenomena. Could it prove that not all theatres are haunted? However, even if Becky was picking up on the residual energy of the fireman and if he was still alive, under the residual energy law there still is a possibility that his image could be witnessed walking his old stomping ground.

Becky – Walking around, we found that we were picking up mostly the residual energy of the theatre rather than any spirit activity. I did manage to validate one of the previous firemen. A technician, who knew the man in question, confirmed my description exactly.

The Victoria Apollo

A Brief History
A vast stretch of open fields, pastures and old pathways existed on the site of the Apollo in 1692. In 1723, Chelsea waterworks was built on the site of the Victoria Station and near the present theatre. The waterworks not only supplied water to the growing population, but also fed irrigation channels to vast reed beds which in 1829 became the world's first public reservoir purification system. The eighteenth century saw the construction of a number of the main roads

that still exist today. Pimlico, as Victoria was previously called, nursed many of the capital's market gardens. A theatre and cinema on the site can be traced back to as early as 1919, when it was called the 'picture theatre'. Due to the urbanisation of London and the completion of Victoria Station in 1861, the building nestled in amongst shops and small businesses. Mirroring Victoria of the twenty-first century, the area was a hive of activity; the current building was built in 1930 as a 'super cinema', a variety theatre specifically designed to facilitate stage shows. It has been a theatre ever since.

The Victoria Apollo Interviews

Cathy O'Rourke was head cleaner at the theatre and worked in the building for the past twenty-five years. She has lots of ghostly tales and has experienced foreboding feelings, especially in one of the hospitality rooms. Cathy said, 'I get pushed and if I stand by the sink, I always sense that someone is standing behind me. I feel like I have come into their territory, they either don't want me here or just want me to go away'. Another area Cathy does not like to go is in the basement, under the stage, 'It's very cold and I get a terrible sad feeling there. I walk through it very quickly because again I have a feeling I'm being followed'. Cathy has heard and seen many things, 'A little girl was seen during the run of *Starlight Express*. We had a bridge that crossed the set and in the middle of the show; the girl, who looked a bit like Shirley Temple, was seen standing on it. The show was stopped and the bridge was investigated. The girl was gone'.

Keith is one of the stage doormen and night security staff. During the running of *Starlight Express* Keith experienced something strange. It was 3 a.m. and Keith had heard a crashing sound coming from the auditorium. As he investigated he noticed a man sitting in Row Q of the stalls. The man was just staring at the stage. Keith recalls exactly what the man looked like, 'The man was in his fifties and bald. He was dressed in black but had a white shirt on. The strangest thing was, although it was quite dark, the man seemed to glow!' Keith challenged the

The Victoria Apollo

man; he shouted at him and told him he shouldn't be in the theatre at this time. The man then got up and proceeded to walk towards the back of the auditorium. Keith followed but the man vanished into thin air. Keith reports that, spookily, the man walked robotically away not unlike a zombie from a horror movie.

An actress from one of the previous shows, *Saturday Night Fever*, retold a story that the building is built on a cemetery. This we believe to be a myth: there are no records that a graveyard or burial plot existed on the at all.

'There are definitely strange things going on in this building', says Paul Barrett. He has been working at the Apollo for the past fifteen years. Starting as an usher and working up to stage door/ night security, Paul does not jump to the paranormal conclusion very easily but there are some things he cannot explain. He recalls that he occasionally sees orbs rushing around the auditorium at night.

Amazingly, Paul has seen the same apparition as his colleague Keith. Once again he was brought to the attention of the auditorium when loud bangs were heard early one morning. He ran into the auditorium and was surprised to see a bald-headed man sitting in Row Q of the stalls. Just like Keith, he shouted out. The man stood up and looked straight at him, then walked up the centre aisle and disappeared. Paul says the man looked very lost and lonely.

Another active area is the pass door to the stage on the auditorium left. Paul tells of a strange humanoid figure 'shooting up' the aisle. During the run of *Starlight Express*, so frequent was this spook that he was given a name 'Squeaky', so-called because of the sound he made as he fled from the cleaners!

Actress and dancer Lisa Cook worked on *Starlight Express* in 2001. One night after the show, she had an audible encounter:

> Everyone had gone home and I was going out that night, so I stayed on to get ready. I left my dressing room and headed down to the stage door by the lift. Then I heard a woman laughing, quite loudly. I was very scared as I knew everyone had left the building. For the year I was there, I noticed oppression in the air; my friend became very depressed and suffered panic attacks.

Jonathon Tucker has been working at the Apollo for the past twelve years and like the others has witnessed a strange man wandering around the auditorium. He has also been hit on the back several times whilst standing at the back of the circle. Jonathon thinks the odd feelings may have something to do with an alleged underground stream that runs beneath the theatre.

An actress who played one of the main characters from *Starlight* had a strange and frustrating experience during one of her songs. Suddenly she heard groaning from the dress circle. This happened on countless occasions and was investigated. They could find no explanation. Another security man whilst on his nightly rounds witnessed some of the seats in the auditorium flapping up and down. He was scared beyond belief.

The Victoria Apollo Investigation

Location: The white VIP room

Reported activity: The ghost of an usher/a presence, feeling you are being watched/cold spots
Investigation: Ian clairvoyantly saw an uptight man who was dressed as a butler/usher. He looked very stern upon entering the room. He felt the team were trespassing on his territory. During a séance, Becky immediately sensed the atmosphere change to an oppressed feeling. She also felt a man's energy but accompanying him were two females. 'There are two women with him also, but they don't stay in this room, they only come in and to make fun of him? They tend to run around on stage a lot because there's more energy on stage'. Becky felt the man, did not like the

team trespassing on his environment She recalled the man was not responsible for the foreboding feelings. He told her the cause was downstairs and it was not a person.

Location: The auditorium
Reported activity: Apparitions of little girl, man seated in stalls, strange creature called 'Squeaky'
Investigation: They discovered a wall of electrical energy by Row X of the stalls. Becky grabbed her dousing rods, and suggested that there is a ley line running under or near the building, which also crosses running water, like an underground stream. This allegedly can cause a tremendous amount of paranormal activity. It is also suggested that, when a massive negative event occurs on a Ley line (the Blitz, explosions, fire and loss of life, for example) it can turn the ley into what is known as a 'black stream' causing the site to become negative, which in turn attracts further negative energy. Is this why there have been many reports of people feeling unpleasant and oppressive? Fact: *The Buckingham Palace ley line' is said to run nearby. The ley line runs from Charing Cross through Victoria. It has also been confirmed that there is a stream beneath the theatre.*

Several digital camera batteries began to fail and a mobile phone rang – no one was on the other end. This is often seen as a possible sign that the energy is being drained by an external force, which is prerequisite to paranormal activity. Becky also felt the whole area was witness to a massive loss of life in a very short space of time, and had something to do with the Second World War. Ian sensed the energies of a young soldier called 'Charlie boy' who died from a shrapnel wound during an explosion. At this time, Ian, alongside a fellow team member, witnessed a little, white light anomaly disappear behind one of the seats. It appeared solid and about 2in in size. There is a rumour that during the Blitz the residents of Victoria suffered an amazing loss of life. Allegedly, all the local hospitals could not cope and the theatre was used as a temporary morgue. This cannot be validated.

Becky suggested that the team perform a spirit release ceremony in order to cleanse the area and help the grounded spirits trapped within the theatre. The mood became very emotional and sad as the emanations of the past event come flooding back. Most of the team perceived all sorts of characters as they passed into the light. The team saw the spirits of ladies with children, and soldiers all patiently waiting in line.

Conclusion   Haunted Scale: 9.5-10
Ian – A worthy investigation. The theatre is riddled with alleged ghosts and haunted to a certain degree. However, I feel that residual energy, our own psychic energy and group neurosis was responsible for sightings of trapped spirits, feelings of sad emotion and light anomalies within the building. I am still incredibly fascinated by the energy given off by ley lines and will keep an open mind about them affecting people's health. The unpleasant feelings, oppression and even sensing you are not alone, can be one of the symptoms of infrasound. It is said that the vibration caused by constant running water against a hard surface can cause a low frequency akin to infrasound. Infrasound is associated with 20hz, below the frequency of human hearing, and is said to cause anxiety, presences and extreme sadness. Is this hidden river or water course beneath the theatre the true explanation of the haunting? An interesting fact I later discovered was that there had been occasional reports of tramps managing to get into the building a night. Could this be an explanation for the sighting of the zombie-like man in Row Q? We also discovered that an unfortunate man suffered a fatal heart attack during a past performance. He was sitting in Row Q. As for the 'Squeaky' the ghost, I remain baffled.

Becky – I felt the man in the VIP room was stuck in a timeline (similar to the effect of a stuck record) but the confusing thing was, I felt he was interacting with us, which is unusual. When sitting in the auditorium, it became very clear to me that there were many souls in need of rescue. I did this by building a bridge between the two worlds and making a light tube for the spirits to transform their energy to the next dimension. If a large group of people have perished in a disaster, one strong character will normally take the lead and others will follow. I popped back a few weeks later and was pleased to notice how light the building seemed.

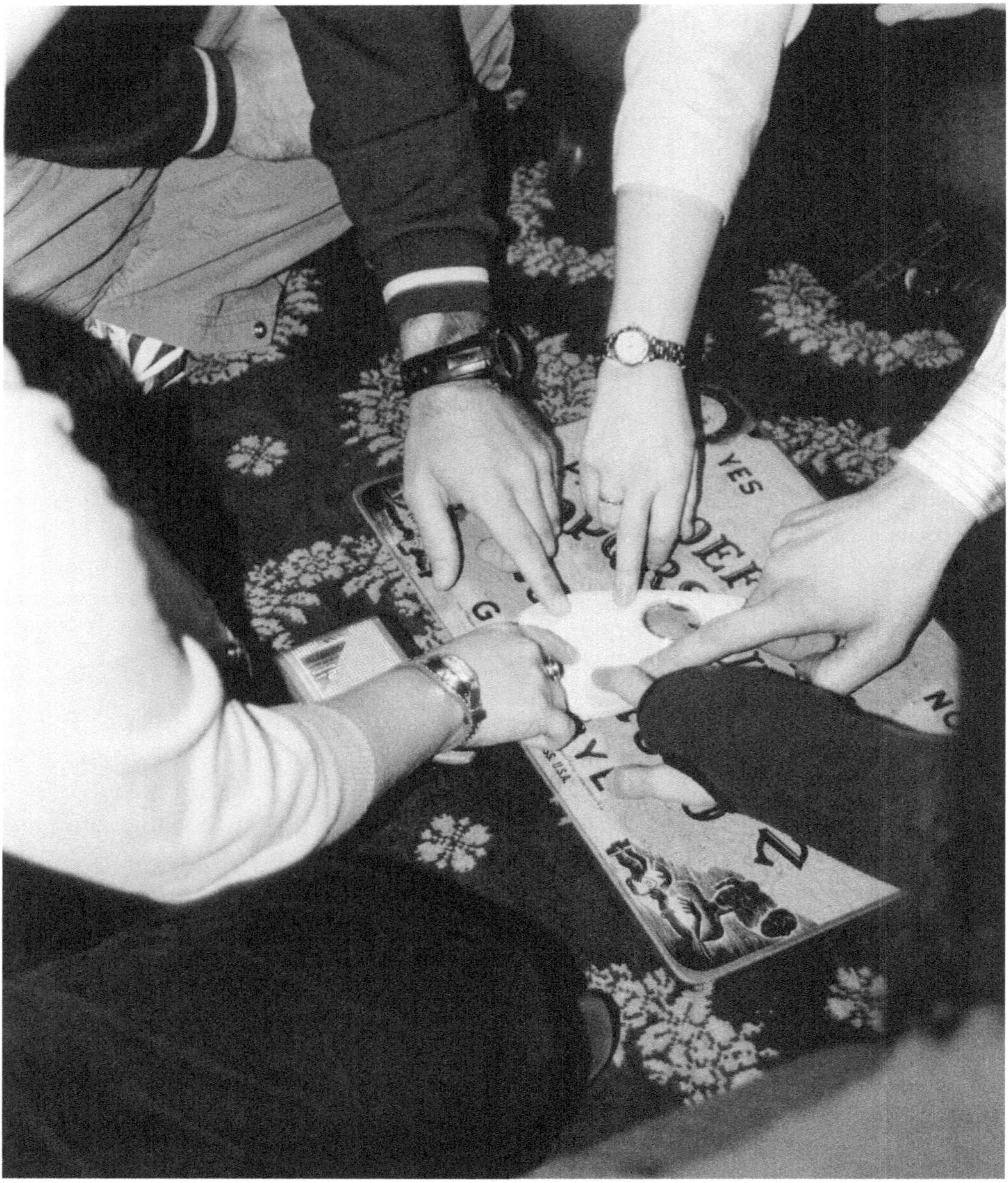

The team contact the ghost of Evelyn Laye at the Piccadilly Theatre.

A story recalls a man who hanged himself here, the boiler room, Trafalger Studios.

Light anomaly or dust particle? St Martin's Theatre, auditorium.

Above: *The team hold a séance in the white room at the Victoria Apollo.*

Left: *Has the image of Freddie Mercury been witnessed in the wings of the Dominion Theatre?*

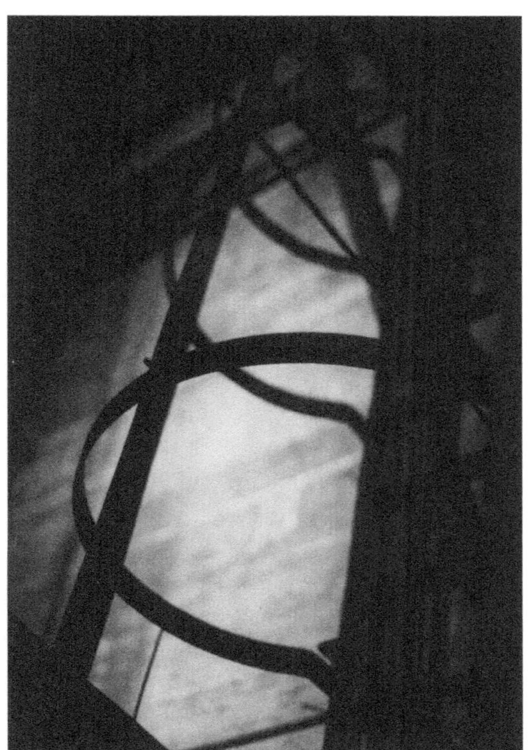

Shadows have been seen moving around the Dominion Theatre's Jacobs ladder.

A white light has been seen gliding down the run at the back of the Phoenix Theatre.

Light anomaly, main theatre

A white figure has been seen standing here at the back of the Victoria Palace auditorium.

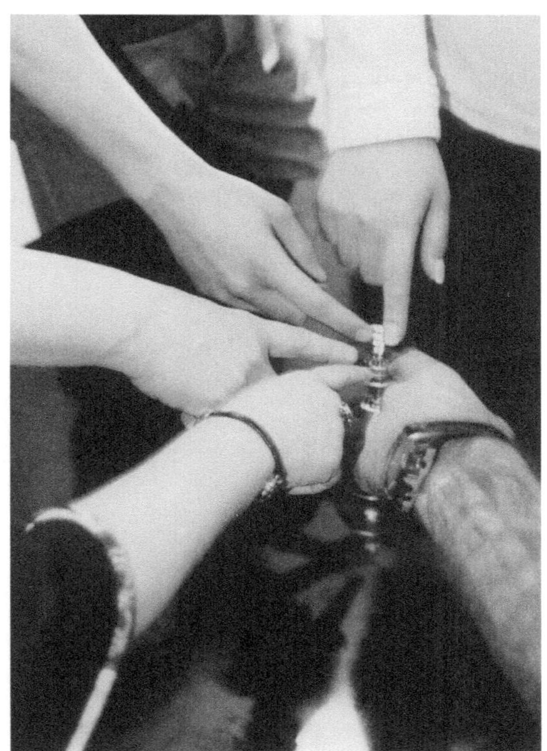

Glass divination at The Queens Theatre

Staff at The Queens theatre have reported white mists floating down this corridor.

Above: *Actor Brian Connelly encountered two blue lights floating at the back of the auditorium of the Victoria Palace.*

Left: *The Shaftesbury theatre is situated on one of the capital's oldest thoroughfares.*

A mysterious Grey Phantom has been seen walking the front of house of the Queens Theatre.

Becky: *It felt like someone was pushing my stomach, backstage at the Shaftesbury Theatre.*

The Dominion Theatre's dressing room 27 is home to violent poltergeist activity.

A Victorian girl was seen on the staircase leading up the fly tower at the Dominion Theatre.

Right: *The ghost of an elderly man haunts this box at the Theatre Royal Haymarket.*

Below left: *The atmosphere changes as Ian and Becky hold vigil in the Phoenix Theatre.*

Below right: *Whilst locking up one night, the Queens Theatre fireman heard a terrifying voice shouting up from the stairs.*

Cambridge Theatre

Could this relatively new theatre be haunted? Caroline Francis was one of the wardrobe staff during the run of *Jerry Springer: The Musical* and was often alone in the mornings. She regularly heard footsteps coming from an empty stairwell or occasional doors slamming. Caroline was shocked to discover the building was empty. A psychic recently suggested the ghost of an old crew member was responsible. The Cambridge is built on the site and epicentre of the slums and 'rookeries of St Giles'. According to our own belief system, energy cannot be destroyed and all the suffering associated with the inhabitants of this slum would have soaked into the ether. Do the faint footsteps and slamming doors belong to the past? Are they just audio replays?

The Aldwych Theatre

The Aldwych Theatre lies in the southern shadow of the Theatre Royal Drury Lane. The name Aldwych derives from the old English word for old. *Eald* and *Wych* are Saxon words for farmstead. The street plan we see today was created by the late Victorian massive redevelopment scheme which was established from a sprawling mass of slums.

Drury Lane, which runs alongside the building, has been an ancient thoroughfare for over 1,000 years. It was recorded in 1199 as the 'Old Way'. In the early sixteenth century it was known as Fortescu Lane. The road became known as Drury Lane in the late sixteenth century when the Drury family built a typical Elizabethan manor house near the site.

By 1737 the area was full of over-populated housing, toxic-smelling industries and timbered buildings that overshadowed small courts and alleyways. Nearby, an iron foundry spewed out pollution. The Aldwych Theatre was built by actor-manager Seymour Hicks and opened in 1905. From 1925-1933, the theatre was made famous for its presentation of a series of farces. *The Aldwych Farces*, as it became known, had the audiences rolling about in the aisles. During the Second World War, the theatre nicknamed the 'escapism theatre' survived the nightly Blitz with mild structural damage.

The Aldwych Interviews

The Aldwych's duty manager, Ruth Slaney-Ambridge has been working at the theatre for seven years, working her way up the ranks from stage-door keeper. It was when she was working at stage door that strange things started to happen. The phones would often ring when no one was there, but this only happened when she was working. She regularly felt presences in the theatre, even though she was alone. Ruth says she could even feel cold spots yet she did not feel scared or threatened.

According to Ruth, the most active area in the building is the stalls bar. The majority of the theatre is built underground with the stage situated almost two levels down from street level. This can naturally feel oppressive from a psychological point of view. In fact the theatre is so deep that there are constant problems with the rising water table. The water is said to come from the Fleet, one of London's lost rivers. 'The stalls bar feels strange, the atmosphere, dense', Ruth claims. 'There have been many accounts of glasses being knocked over and people being touched'.

Another active area is the auditorium where there have been many reports of spirit lights and orbs, chills in the air, and movement in the stalls. This phenomenon is reported to happen when the theatre is empty. The back of dress circle, the upper circle and auditorium right are also regular locations for countless reports of activity.

The Aldwych Theatre

Jorge Tell, head usher at the theatre, explains there is another area front of house that has been reported to have activity. Several cleaners have heard strange noises by the manager's offices. One day a Brazilian cleaner saw a door open on its own; she ran away and they never saw her again. Jorge also recounts an event ten years ago, 'an usher was sitting watching the show when she heard a woman crying from over her shoulder. When they turned around, they were shocked to find no one there'.

The Aldwych Investigation

Location: The stalls bar
Reported activity: General poltergeist activity
Investigation: With a television switched onto white noise, the team wanted to try an experiment in a modern version of scrying. Becky stared into the TV and clairvoyantly saw lots of people dancing within the fuzz but felt drawn to an industrial era, 'I have the impression that there was an industrial centre here'. *Fact: During the industrial expansion of London, there was an iron-works factory nearby.*

Becky sensed a male presence by the bar, 'He's not here very often but he moves things, turns things off or shifts things. It's not threatening, it's just his sense of humour, he stands with his elbows on the bar and watches and laughs'. *Fact: Glasses have allegedly been knocked off the shelf behind the bar.* 'He's got an extremely shocked look on his face, because he knows I can see him. I feel he was involved in a bar fight and was strangled. He's a rough bloke and a real cockney geezer'. Actress Julie Stark, who joined the team, who was left alone in the bar reported, 'It was a bit odd when the telly turned itself off and then I got really hot, really hot, but there was clanking noises from behind the door. It was truly scary'.

Location: Auditorium
Reported activity: Light anomalies, cold spots and psychic breezes
Investigation: Becky tuned in:

> I can see a guy who looks like he's dressed like Willy Wonka. He has a top hat, cane. He was a male entrepreneur who owned a vast amount of this area; he had lots of money and transformed this building to what it is now. But the weird thing is, I feel his clothing looks wrong for the time period. I can't place it properly. I feel he was just wildly eccentric, this [theatre] was his baby but then I am seeing him walk out of here for the last time because he sold it.

Fact: We are later shown a photograph of theatre actor-manager, Seymour Hicks. Ironically, he is dressed in a costume that resembles Johnny Depp's costume for Willy Wonka. Seymour was a very important character in the creation of the West End theatre we see today.

The team spot several red light anomalies in the auditorium and hear unexplainable noises. Upon leaving the auditorium, the team are taken down through the orchestra pit, into a large void underneath sub-stage and discover an underground stream. Pete the electrician informs the team it is one of London's lost rivers. Becky is convinced this is the reason for so much activity in the building.

Conclusion   Haunted Scale: 8.5–10

Ian – I felt the investigation of the Aldwych theatre produced some rewarding activity. The confirmation of Becky's description of Seymour Hicks is a great example of psychic skills at their best. If we were to consider visitation by his spirit a possibility, then this theatre would definitely be a very favourable place for the theatre manger to return to. I felt that all the light anomalies witnessed were displaced psychic energy, a result of the evening's energetic performance mixed with the vast amount of electrical power. This is similar to what happens in an electrical storm with the sudden appearance of lightning. The lone vigil experiment worked to a certain extent. Being alone in an alleged haunted room psychologically plays with the mind. The noises heard could just be natural and only highlighted by hypersensitivity. I later discovered that most televisions, when tuned into white noise, can turn themselves off after twenty minutes. This was well within the time of the lone vigil and therefore cannot be conclusive paranormal evidence. Once again we have to look at the fact that the theatre has an underground stream running beneath the building. Could infrasound associated with the frequency of the running water cause the phenomena in this building? I would love to investigate this theatre further.

Becky – Imagination is the chalk board that spirit writes on. When I was describing a man who looked like Willy Wonka I was surprised by the kind of photographic validation that was shown to us. It always gives me a real rush of excitement when this kind of evidence is found. This theatre is haunted!

The Prince Edward Theatre

Mark McGuinness, who works as an usher, retold the story of the ghost of the pink lady, 'A ballerina once threw herself off the Grand Circle and was said to be responsible for activity in the Grand Circle box. There have been several accounts of having the feeling that someone is playing with your hair or breathing on your neck'. This particular story does not seem to run alongside the building's history. The theatre opened in 1930 with a musical but was converted into a dance and cabaret hall five years later. The building has had many guises since then ranging from a casino to a cinema, eventually returning to a theatre in 1975. Research has failed to come up with a ballet performed at the theatre. Could this ghost be a myth?

St Martins Theatre

A Brief History

In 1682, Newport House stood on the site of the theatre. The house was adjacent to the rambling Cock and Pye fields. A path twists and turns north through hedged countryside and pathways passing through the tiny hamlets of the future city. The only sound is the wind and the birds. Over 300 years later, the noise is deafening. The modern streets fork out in acute angles as thousands of souls walk anonymously to their destinations, avoiding eye contact, avoiding touch.

During the eighteenth and nineteenth centuries, the site of the theatre was situated south of the parish of St Giles and a stone's throw from the infamous 'Rookery'. The area was a honeycomb of alleys, dirt and distemper yet was a favourable home for porters, stage hands and Irish immigrants who fled the famine and poverty in Ireland. After the mass clean-up in the early twentieth century, the theatre was built by Lord Willoughby de Broke in a fine example of Georgian architecture. St Martins is described as the capital's most attractive small theatre. The theatre finally opened in 1916 due to it being delayed by the beginning of the Second World War.

It was in 1974, when Ambassadors Theatre transferred its successful hit to the stage of the St Martins, that theatre history take place. *The Mousetrap* by Agatha Christie is the world's longest running play. At the time of writing the show has run for fifty-three years. Incidentally, the prop revolver used in the show is now housed in the Victoria & Albert Museum, whilst the original clock still ticks on the mantelpiece of the original set.

The St Martins Theatre Investigation

Location: Foyer and family room

Reported activity: None

Investigation: Both Becky and Ian independently witnessed the image of an usher or butler standing to one side. He is dressed in traditional twentieth-century period garments, with a white shirt or jacket and slicked backed hair. In the family room, Becky senses an aristocratic lady whose clothing seems older than the theatre itself, 'I'm picking up on a woman, very grandiose. Somebody's obviously very theatrical, and [has] a real flair about them'. Spookily, she describes exactly the portrait of a lady which hangs in one of the corridors. The portraits, among many others, originate from the ancestral home of the family who used to own the building. According to research, the family lost their home in death duties and the art now hangs in the theatre. Did Becky sense the spirit of this lady? Is it possible that a spirit can attach itself to a painting?

Location: The set of *The Mousetrap*
Reported activity: None
Investigation: The temperature suddenly dropped, as they sat on the prop sofa in darkness. Ian captured a wonderful light anomaly. Becky sensed a lovely old spirit lady, 'There's an old lady who used to be in this show, she still frequents it and comes into say hello. I see a short lady, about 5ft 4in, round, and has got curly brown hair'. The atmosphere changed and a presence was felt by the team. 'Right in front of me, I really don't like it. That's the first time someone's actually scared me. They just keep getting in my face, a big bloke, and he came right up to me in my face'. The team felt intense cold air and tingling sensations on their heads.

Conclusion   Haunted Scale: 3-10
Ian – If we imagine residual energies like layers on a cake, we can almost understand how different ages of residual apparitions are seen. On the modern ground level, we witnessed a fairly modern residual ghost. As we descended into the strata of the theatre, Becky sensed much older ghosts. Most stages and auditoriums are built deep into the ground, in most cases at the same level as ancient time frames. Was the aggressive male energy the residue of one of the Rookery's notorious residents? On the other hand, the stage felt very menacing but was this due to a psychological reaction to the team being in complete darkness? Once again, hypersensitivity to breezes and electrical energy can manipulate the mind to overreact and cause an adrenalin rush, which in turn triggers a fight or flight reaction.

Becky – Psychics are open to the possibility of psychic attack from the energy of the living, and also spirit. It is unlikely anything can truly harm you. I have never been spooked before by spirit, but that spirit on the stage had it in mind to spook me, and being in the dark in a space I had not seen before, I'm not surprised I was a little freaked out.

The Trafalgar Studios

A Brief History

Beyond the pastures and farmland of Tudor London, the Whitehall Palace spread over the future site of the theatre. As extensive as Whitehall today, and covering 23 acres, the palace was one of the biggest, distinguished dwellings of the period and home to King Henry VIII, Cardinal Wolsey, and Charles II. In 1691, fire destroyed most of the palace apart from its banqueting hall, which still can be visited today.

One of the first ever Elizabethan playhouses to be built was also called the Whitehall Theatre (it stood further along down the road from the Trafalgar Studios). The area was also infamous for executions. King Charles I was beheaded outside nearby Banqueting House and public executions were commonplace in Charing Cross (a stone's throw from the site). From 1650-1930, the Old Ship Tavern stood on the former site of the Trafalgar Studios. The tavern backed on to the famous seventeenth-century spring gardens or the pleasure gardens as it was also known. The foundations of the tavern are found hidden deep within the bowels of the theatre. In 1930, with the inn demolished, the Whitehall Theatre was built on the vacant site.

The theatre opened on 29 September 1930 and built up a good reputation for producing popular comedies but as the Second World War started, revue shows were born in response to the wanton escapism. The building has been closed and refurbished several times in between being used as an exhibition for memorabilia from the two world wars, and more recently became a TV studio. After major refurbishment in 2005, the Trafalgar Studios were born.

The Trafalgar Studios

The Trafalgar Studios Interview

Ben Evans is the technical manager at the Trafalgar and is aware of one particular story which could result in a ghost sighting. He said, 'About twenty-odd years ago, a maintenance man walked in to the noisy boiler room and hung himself. There has been no particular sightings of his ghost but the room does look like a place a ghost would like to live'.

Below ground level lies one of the theatre bars. 'This has terrible cold spots', says Ben. He then remembered another room which has a strange feeling attached to it, the theatre's electrical supply room (amp room):

Now, I don't like it at all. It is the one place I cannot go, look, up there. There's something about it. When I switch off last thing at night, I just feel something is watching me from up there. When I'm in here, it doesn't feel human.

The Trafalgar Investigation
Location: The boiler room
Reported activity: None
Investigation: Straight away, one of the team senses the residual energy of an old man in a brown overall. Becky felt his weight caused a back injury, 'I felt this man is one dimensional rather than two-dimensional and part of the wall absorption. I feel we have been joined by another spirit, a taller chap, from a different time period but I don't think he is anything connected with this room'. I think he is just listening and observing.

Location: Amp room
Reported activity: Strange atmosphere/sense that there is something watching
Investigation: The room which houses the theatre's main electricity supply is small A tiny mezzanine floor was originally part of the old staircase of the Ship Tavern. Becky noticed something on the mezzanine, 'I feel there is a little entity up there, it looks a bit like Gollum and seems to be feeding off the electricity, and I can see him. It's naked, it is very skinny, and it's got really weird eyes, a very gaunt, longish face. It's not human or ever has been. Do you ever have random drops in power?' It is confirmed the building suffers from multiple power cuts and blown light bulbs. When taking a photograph of the suspected area, we noticed an obscure green blob in the frame.

Conclusion   Haunted Scale: 2–10
Ian – The investigation took place during major refurbishment of the theatre. It has been suggested that building work can have tremendous effect on paranormal activity therefore I was disappointed to discover that during our time in the theatre, it was fairly quiet. If a suicide actually happened in the boiler room it would naturally leave a strong emotional residue. This was not felt by the psychics. However, Becky did start talking about hanging and executions at a later date. The executions were also relevant to the area's past.

In this current climate, it is almost acceptable to assume the existence of ghosts and spirits, but if one was to start talking about non-humans, elementals or extra-terrestrials there is a high possibility we would be ridiculed. The existence of such entities has been around for thousands of years, yet the belief in them even splits the spiritual community in half. Personally I remain on the fence. I felt the energy and odd feelings associated within the amp room are purely due to the vast amount of electrical power housed in the room, and the effect it has on the body's bio-rhythms. However, the constant power cuts and blown light bulbs (sometimes twenty in one day) could be the result of the energy-eating entity, but also the result of a problematic power source. It is interesting that the strange green blob was captured exactly where Becky witnessed the entity, however a digital error or flash reflection cannot be ruled out.

Becky – I was really fascinated with what we found at this theatre. The creature who looked like Gollum was living off the electrical energy in the amp room. This entity exists on a lower level of vibration. If we look at photographs of lightening storms, the electricity is often shown as a green energy and I felt the entity could not exist without the power and energy it fed on. This is why, when photographed, it was portrayed as a green energy. This brilliant evidence is validated by the power drops in the theatre and vast amount of blown light bulbs.

The Old Vic Theatre

A Brief History

Some of the stone from the Old Vic derives from the original Savoy Hospital which was established in 1509. Built in 1818, The Royal Colburg's (as it was known then) opening night included a melodrama, an Asiatic ballet and a harlequinade. Unfortunately, a short time later, it closed.

For one Victorian woman, the depravity associated with the local poor was totally uncontrollable, therefore she decided to do something about it. In 1880, Miss Emma Cons was a leading Victorian reformer who owned much of the property around Waterloo. She reopened the theatre as The Royal Victoria Coffee & Music Hall in order to give the locals an alternative place to go over the weekend. The popular shows put together on a shoestring were hard work to organise so Miss Cons asked her niece, Lillian Baylis to come over from South Africa and lend a hand. Lillian was one of the first greatest pioneers of British theatre and when her aunt died in 1912 she took over the management of the theatre. Lillian was also famous for introducing the lower classes to theatre. She totally believed that the power of theatre enriched the lives of the poor. By 1912 she was putting on Shakespeare for the residents of Waterloo. Almost immediately The Vic became the people's theatre. Lillian eventually died in 1937. In 1941, the theatre was damaged by enemy bombing and for nine years remained closed. It opened again in the 1950s offering seasons of Shakespeare and traditional theatre.

The Old Vic Theatre Interviews

The theatre is rumoured to house a couple of resident ghosts and it comes as no surprise to find they are reported to be the spirits of Lillian Baylis and Emma Cons.

Ned Sego has been the stage doorman for many years and knows the building like the back of his hand. One evening he followed an actress who he believed to be part of a visiting company down a corridor. She first appeared to him on the second floor as he was locking up the theatre. Ned just assumed she was lost. He noticed she was wearing period clothing but thought nothing of it as this was commonplace in a theatre. With the lady at a short distance Ned followed her further until she disappeared around a corner. Ned declares, 'She was as clear as you stand in front of me today. As I came down the stairs to let her out, she disappeared through that bricked-up door way. My heart stopped; it was terrifying to see a solid figure walk through a wall'. This apparition has been seen several times over the years. Dressed in period costume, she clasps her bloodstained hands to her chest – it is said the blood is fake and the lady is the spirit of an actress in an old Shakespearian tragedy.

More recently, during a run of *Hamlet*, several actors noticed a white figure gliding across the back of the stalls. The figure was totally unexplainable. Could this spook be Lillian Baylis, checking up on the house and the quality of drama? For it is rumoured, if the theatre fell into disrepute, she would put a curse on it and haunt it until the end of time.

Ben Evans used to work at the theatre and remembers a story of an old master carpenter. Ben was a firm non-believer until one night he followed a woman who again disappeared into a wall. This scared him so much that he refused to talk about it and he would sack on the spot any crew member who questioned him on the experience.

Andy Sutherland, a former fireman, worked there in the mid-1980s. He, too, told a story of an old master carpenter who saw something, but this time it was the legs of a woman walking up the stairs. Two different accounts, but both very strange indeed. Andy remembers he had multiple sightings and odd feelings whilst locking up.

The Old Vic

Another reported ghost at the Old Vic is the ghost of Eric Moss. It was after the First World War and Eric was due to play Brutus in *Julius Caesar*. Unfortunately this never happened as he, alongside three other members of the cast, died in the 'Spanish flu' epidemic of 1917-1918. In the spirit of showbusiness, the show had to go on and replacements were found. It was only at the end of the performance that things seemed a little strange. Several people asked who the man in the orchard scene was. The director asked his friend in one of the boxes who replied, 'The man on his own? Oh! You mean Eric Moss?' With that, a cold shiver ran down the director's back. Eric had wanted the part so much, he appeared on opening night to make sure everything went well.

Emma Cons is said to haunt the balcony of the upper circle. It is rumoured that she has been seen looking out of the windows onto the small garden over the road. Ned is always the last person to go home, 'It feels great to walk around the auditorium. You hear sounds and it's like the auditorium is talking to you. I have no problem being alone in this theatre. There is so much love attached to it'.

The Old Vic Investigation
Location: Circle bar, front of house
Reported activity: Apparitions in window

Investigation: Becky noticed what seemed to be a tremendous energy rush past her as another team member feels energy, 'I'm picking up on a woman who looks very motherly, she's smiling at us. She is over there now. She is not saying anything'. Becky sensed another female energy but is confused, 'Is she someone from long ago or am I seeing a modern lady in a period costume?' Could this be the ghost of the actress in period clothing?

Location: Auditorium
Reported activity: White apparitions, feelings of love and contentment
Investigation: Becky residually picked up a name, 'I've been given the name Margaret', and feels it is very important to the building. Could it be Margaret Leighton (1922-1976), an English actress who became a star of the Old Vic many years ago? Psychic artist James was brought in to capture the alleged ghosts in pen and ink. He sketched a face which looked uncannily like Miss Emma Cons.

Conclusion   Haunted Scale: 4-10
Ian – I felt the theatre was haunted more by memories rather than any ghosts. It is good to feel that residual energy can also be positive and have a warm and calming effect as well as negative and uncomfortable. Should the spirit of Emma and Lillian want to visit the earth plane, then this would be the place. I feel it could be possible to perceive or sense the imprint of these wonderful caring ladies. The ghost of the blood-soaked lady baffles me a little. Actors, especially method actors, can inject a tremendous amount of emotional energy into a role, and if this is repeated for a considerable time, the after-effect could cause a residual haunting. However, why does she walk through a wall? If this was a residual haunting, the wall through which the ghost walks must be a recent addition. If we were to look at old plans of the building, we should find a corridor or door in place of the wall. The results of the psychic art experiment were remarkable. We did manage to locate a painting of Emma Cons and the likeness is uncanny. However, it is not proof that Emma's Spirit was present at the investigation. The fact that an artist can draw the dead, whether that be that from residual energy or actual spirit communication, is still incredibly paranormal.

Becky – I do not feel Emma Cons' ghost is resident at this theatre, but I feel her spirit pops in from time to time to keep her eye on the place. It was her passion and vision. I felt the theatre had an interesting vibration, with a lot of movement. There was a great deal of love and attitude attached to the building and this has carried on over the decades. You can feel that the enthusiasm emanating from the atmosphere. I picked up on a variety of actors, but the energy of the actress who reminded me of one of the Redgrave sisters was very strong. I felt she died young and had a habit of fainting due to a restricted corseted costume.

Her Majesty's Theatre

This theatre is the fourth building to be built on this site. The original was called The Queens Theatre and opened in 1705. The apparition of the actor-manager Sir Herbert Beerbohm-Tree, who worked at the theatre in 1897, has been seen on countless occasions. This alleged haunting has all the hallmarks of the residual replay. Take an actor-manager, a whole lot of passion and hard graft and you will have enough energy and emotion to stain the atmosphere. In fifty years' time, will the ghosts of the present theatre managers haunt the corridors of the future buildings? This theatre is grouped alongside some of the capital's oldest theatres and yet we find very few ghost stories. Maybe history and ghosts do not go hand-in-hand as we had originally thought.

Her Majesty's Theatre

The Queens Theatre

The Queens Theatre

A Brief History

Originally countryside, the Queens Theatre is built on one of the earliest inhabited parts of London's Soho. A number of small cottages and farm buildings were dotted down Coleman Hedge Lane (Wardour Street) as it intercepted fields and pastures.

With the population explosion of London, this area was soon full of residential housing and small businesses. Furniture, silverware, leatherwear and glassware were abundant and thrived for many decades. By 1813, six properties lay on the theatre's site; most were small shops and boarding houses. Above eye-level, most of the buildings in Soho have not changed for several hundred years as most of the historic buildings still retain the seventeenth-century facades of yesteryear. It was not until the tenements were knocked down in the nineteenth century and Shaftesbury Avenue was sculptured into the landscape that the skyline changed.

The Queens Theatre was built as an exact copy of the Gielgud theatre (previously known as the Globe) and opened in 1907. The Queens, amongst other newly built theatres in the Avenue, entertained the people of London for another thirty-seven years. The Blitz of the Second World War brought devastating change. On Tuesday 24 September 1940, London was suffering from yet another nightly raid of German bombers. Unfortunately, the Queens took a direct hit. A highly explosive device destroyed the front of house but, surprisingly, most of the auditorium and backstage areas remained untouched. It was later discovered that three people died during the attack. The theatre remained in ruins but managed to hire out backstage until it was eventually rebuilt in 1957. The show in residence is *Les Misérables*.

The Queens Interviews

The chief electrician at the Queens Theatre, Mike Cordina has heard many stories about the building's ghosts and has even witnessed an apparition that to this day causes him concern. The theatre was in pre-production for a new play. Everyone had gone home. All the exits doors were locked and chained. The only way out of the theatre was by the stage door. Mike was walking around the front of house by the upper circle, when he noticed a man in front of him. Mike said he looked like a middle-aged man who appeared to be dressed in a long grey coat. Mike cannot remember what specific style it was, although he did notice the coat had velvet lapels and that the man's hair was grey and short.

Mike says:

> The man was walking ahead of me and heading to a dead end. I naturally thought he was one of the many contractors employed by the theatre so I shouted out. The man ignored me and walked around a corner so I followed. To my amazement I reached a dead end only to find no one was there.

Craig Russell was one of the front-of-house staff. He, too, recalls seeing a strange man in upper circle of the auditorium. On a second glance, he was gone. Craig knew the theatre was empty. The man in grey has made regular appearances over the years. The front-of-house staff have reported cold areas and tense foreboding atmospheres. There is even one report of someone seeing a strange white mist in one of the corridors.

One of the members of the cast of *Contact* was on stage during the show. They noticed a lady in the Royal Box. They reported, 'That's not unusual, but the box was closed to the public and full of sound speakers and was promptly investigated but spookily they found no one'.

A duty fireman informed us she was frightened out of her wits one night whilst she had been locking up. 'I was in the stalls when I heard a very a very loud stamping of feet coming from the stalls bar. Reluctantly and terrified I called out. There was no reply. Suddenly someone shouted out in a very deep voice "It's me!" Knowing I was alone in the building, I left as quickly as I could'.

One of the resident shows followspot operators often sees spirit lights flashing around her at the back of the auditorium. The operator, who is definitely a believer, has even heard her name being called by a woman's voice. Back in 1999, Richard Kingcott was working on the *The Lady in the Van* when one day he noticed a man in white – 'it was like a haze of white' – walk down the stage left wing and disappear without a trace. There was no reasonable explanation.

The Queens Investigation

Location: The upper circle, auditorium

Reported activity: Light anomalies, figure of a man, an Edwardian lady

Investigation: Becky sensed a male energy similar to the one she had recently felt. This time she explained what he looks like, 'He's not tall, thin but has a little bit of a tummy. I felt he lost weight before he crossed over. I felt he was a theatre manger or had some sort of managerial job'. With no name it is difficult to validate this.

Location: Upper circle corridor

Reported activity: Strange presences and unnerving feelings

Investigation: Ian captured a large singular light anomaly above one of the team's heads. They decided to experiment with table tilting and glass divination. Almost instantly one of the theatres representatives felt upset. The table started to vibrate a little, as another team member sensed a male energy present. Becky asked out loud, 'Are you grounded here? If so, would you like to be released from the theatre?' The divination revealed that the alleged energy belonged to a man called Mathew who worked at the theatre during the 1940s. It suggested he was gay in life and would seek solace near one of the modern male ushers who incidentally was present at this investigation, and evidently was witness to a number of paranormal goings-on in the theatre. The divination exercise also contacted a female energy who was allegedly killed by the Second World War bomb. The team felt that the lady, who was a nanny called Emily, died immediately in the explosion as her car passed by the theatre. Some of the team members felt very emotional as the circle was closed down.

Conclusion   Haunted Scale: 4-10

Ian – I felt the theatre has lots of residual energy and if one was to surf through that, a number of major characters would stand out. I feel we can sense the more emotional personalities that have lived, worked and died in buildings. Even though the theatre world accepts homosexuality, being gay in the 1940s was definitely taboo and for some a very lonely experience in which the emanations still linger in the very fabric of the building. The divination experiment deduced that the theatre is allegedly haunted by Mathew, the gay ghost. I felt we all were possibly tuning into the residue or stain of this man's energy. Who is to say he did not actually exist, but at present, we cannot find any documented validation. I felt the table tilting and glass divination was not conducive evidence of spirit communication. It is incredibly easy to move the glass subconsciously and table tilting can be executed by a mixture of wanton belief, psychic energy, and subconscious movement scientifically known as involuntary muscular movement. However, in a controlled environment with a physical medium, table tilting can be tangible proof of spirit communication. We must remember, even though the movement may be caused by our own psychic energy as well as the power of the mind, I will class it as an aspect of paranormal phenomena.

Becky – When I was previously working at the Queens Theatre, I would often feel a male spirit come and stand behind me. One day, I asked this spirit for some information about himself and he told me he worked in the office which was situated through the door at the back of the auditorium. This confused me as there was no door there. About a week later, as I left work via front of house, I passed an exhibition of old photos of the theatre. To my amazement, there was an old one of the auditorium and the door the spirit spoke about. I wonder if Mathew was that same man. A short while after the investigation, I returned to the Queens and decided to help him cross over. I asked the spirit team to come and take is hand and guide him to the spirit world. A few moments later the atmosphere changed. I couldn't feel him anymore.

New Ambassadors Theatre

A psychic recently felt this theatre was haunted by a caretaker who passed to spirit sometime in the 1960s. His figure has not been seen but his presence has been felt. Anyone who repeatedly walks the same route or sits in the same seat for years on end can leave a residue of themselves behind. Is this what the psychic tuned in to? Built in 1913 and on the site of the infamous slums of St Giles, do the dark corridors of the theatre withhold the area's gloomy past in its shadows?

The Victoria Palace Theatre

A Brief History

In 1682, the pastures and market gardens around Victoria were known as 'London's pantry'. It was once said that the belly of London was always hungry, and the throat of London thirsty. At this time, the capital's water was not the best thing in the world to drink, so our ancestors found something else to quench their thirst. Beer was plentiful and cheap. Weaker than the beer drunk in today's pubs, it watered the rich and the poor. Breweries sprung up all over the capital. They were large in size and normally contained their own pub. A brewery can be traced on the site of the Victoria Palace as far back as the late 1600s. Centuries later, the pub attached to the brewery was called the Royal Standard Tavern. It was here that a man called Jon Moy first offered an evening of 'select harmonic meetings'. This then developed by way of a programme of concerts and finally into the conventional music hall. It was here, at the back of the tavern, that people performed what was to become *Vaudeville*. In 1911, the present theatre was built. It had become the longest standing music hall in London. In 1934 the theatre changed its name to the Victoria Palace under the management of theatre impresario Seymour Hicks. Today the theatre stands opposite the Victoria Apollo and at the time of writing is showing *Billy Elliot: the Musical*.

The Victoria Palace Interviews

Stage-door keeper Kerry Barona feels the building has a comfortable air about it. Like every doorman in the West End, she has to lock up the building on her own after the evening's performances. 'I do sense energies and feel different presences, but I feel as if I am being looked after'. In contrast, one employee said, 'When I walked through the door for the first time, I didn't feel happy. I found the theatre draining. I didn't feel comfortable in the building, it was not the people or the job – it was the building'.

Helen Bowmer was the wig mistress on *Billy Elliot*. 'I was walking to the wig room, when suddenly I noticed a strange icy breeze rush past my face'. Even though the skylight was open it was a very hot summer's day and there was no breeze. Helen is an open-minded sceptic; she cannot explain the breeze but it spooked her. On another occasion, Helen arrived at work to find the door to the wig room locked, but was informed the door was left open. Frustrated, she then walked back to stage door to get a key only to return to find the door open. There was no one in the building and only one key. Was someone playing a joke? José Rodríguez was also working in the wig room during a run of *Tonight's the Night* and he, too, had trouble with the door. Somehow, once again, it had locked itself. He also recalls witnessing a wig being thrown across the room by unseen hands. There have been numerous accounts of objects moving or being thrown about. Could this be a poltergeist at work?

Not all activity is centred on the wardrobe department. During a rehearsal of *Billy Elliot*, the actor playing young Billy witnessed a strange white figure standing at the back of the auditorium. The theatre was empty.

Actor and comedian Brian Connelly spoke to us about a strange encounter he had during the run of *Jolson*. Brian, who was playing Al Jolson, was onstage with fellow actress Sally Ann Triplet, when he noticed two blue lights floating around the back of the auditorium. Although he found it odd, he never mentioned it to anyone. Then several years later he read an interview with Sally and she also told a story of strange lights at the back of the auditorium. Brian was perplexed, but has one theory. He actually felt the spirit of Jolson himself passed through him onstage. Underneath the stage, there are reports of tense atmospheres, headaches and a feeling of depression. Could all this phenomena be connected?

The Victoria Palace Investigation

Location: Wardrobe corridor
Reported activity: General poltergeist phenomena, psychic breezes
Investigation: The team immediately sensed a young male energy. Becky reported, 'I can really feel something here; someone is running up and down the corridor, banging on all the doors. He is male and young. He has a cracking sense of humour, a real jokester, although I feel I have a weight on my chest'. Ian sensed that the lad was about seventeen and died from tuberculosis which may explain why Becky sensed the chest pain. It was decided that the young lad's energy was residual which emanated from the early Victorian times. He worked in one of the buildings in many guises and originated from a poor background.

Location: Auditorium
Reported activity: Light anomalies
Investigation: A female energy was felt but she is not connected to the theatre. She looked like a bag lady, with long loose clothes, and belonged to the working classes.

Conclusion   Haunted Scale: 1–10
Ian – Was the young tearaway in the wardrobe corridor responsible for the poltergeist activity? The answer is probably no. I felt his energy was purely residual and, even though history informs us that tuberculosis was rife during the last couple of centuries, without a name or date it would prove impossible to validate the young man. In order to look for the culprits for the poltergeist phenomena, I feel we have to look at various natural energy factors. Pure and simple psychic energy expelled from the emotional outbursts of employees, electrical voltage housed within

The Victoria Palace

the theatre, and possible ley lines near the building could all fuse together and create a huge energy force. Can this sometimes overload and cause sparks of poltergeist activity? As with most haunted locations there is never one simple explanation. One interesting fact refers back to the hormonal teenager as the cause for poltergeist activity. It is suggested that the chemical reactions of puberty can result in poltergeist infestation and is documented in many cases. *Billy Elliot* is full of young teenagers – are they responsible?

Becky – I did expect to feel more energy at the Victoria Palace. I was very happy that we tuned into the boy on the stairs. One thing I have found with most theatre staff is that they are happy to work with and around the spirits and do not feel and fear for them at all. I think this is wonderful and just goes to show that most theatre people have a deep understanding of the paranormal.

The Savoy Theatre

The theatre was built in 1881 on the site of the old Savoy Palace which was established in the early thirteenth century. The Savoy was the first ever theatre in the world to be lit by electricity. Poltergeist activity has been fairly prevalent in the wardrobe department. Could the inhabitants of the old palace still roam the defunct corridors? Or is the reported activity easily explainable as natural phenomena?

The Comedy Theatre

Ex-theatre manger Simon Francis was locking-up one night and was incredibly spooked to see a large shadow of a man in a top hat looming over him. This theatre was built in 1881, when top hats were worn by upper-class gentlemen to many social gatherings. Ghosts are often perceived as shadows, sometimes stationary, sometimes moving.

The Piccadilly Theatre

As early as 1739, there have been stables on the site of the Piccadilly Theatre supplying all the traders to Soho with hay and water. By the nineteenth century, south-west Soho was one of the most squalid parts of London, yet the rich of Piccadilly lived in grandeur only a few streets away.

In 1928, the now-vacant plot was bought by the Piccadilly Theatre Co. The position was not favourable but the rent was cheap. The company wanted to build a theatre of their own and in 1928 the Piccadilly Theatre opened with the play *Blue Eyes* starring Evelyn Laye who was one of Britain's most acclaimed actresses. That same year, the theatre also became a cinema and premiered *The Singing Fool* starring Al Jolson which, incidentally, was the first ever talking picture to be shown in Britain.

Finally in 1929, the Piccadilly returned to its original role as a theatre and went on to present a variety of stage entertainment ranging from drama to comedy, musicals to Shakespeare. In 1942 *Macbeth* opened, starring Sir John Geilgud. The theatrical superstition attached to the play was said to be responsible for the unsuccessful run. In 1943, the curse of *Macbeth* was blamed for a flying bomb attack. The theatre was badly damaged and closed until the war was over.

The Piccadilly Theatre Interviews

One of the cast members from the current show (at the time of writing) *Guys and Dolls* was keen to tell her story. One particular night she was underneath the stage when suddenly she felt a strange sensation. She felt she was being pushed forward by an invisible force. So strong was this push, it spooked her terribly. The actress reported she has felt it before on numerous occasions, mainly in the wing by prompt corner, but this time the odd force seemed to pull her backwards. She felt as if she was standing on balls which made her roll backwards. Alongside this feeling, she immediately smelt what can be only described as stale water – the sort you get in a vase of flowers.

Stephen, the duty manger has also been pushed. This time, it was in one of the back staircases, front of house. He said he felt a hand on his arm. Stephen sensed no threat but was a little alarmed. Stephen assumed it was the ghost of actress Evelyn Lay, who was rumoured to haunt the Piccadilly.

Jamie, one of the stage doormen, is a believer. When he is alone locking up the building at night, he has seen and heard doors closing. Strange noises are said to echo down the corridors. He, too, wondered whether it was the ghost of Evelyn.

Rumours of the theatre's resident ghost are all over the West End. Almost everyone we spoke to at the Piccadilly told this story:

> One day a portrait of Evelyn was taken down and stored in the offices. From that that day, things started going wrong in the theatre. It was said that the spirit of Evelyn was upset that her picture had been removed. Once the painting had been put back, all was quiet.

The Piccadilly Theatre

The Piccadilly Investigation

Location: Auditorium

Reported activity: Pushing and shoving, basic poltergeist phenomena

Investigation: The team decided to use a traditional Ouija board during this investigation. Becky had trouble breathing, '[What] I am feeling is a sort of compression on the chest, like I can't breath'. *Fact: She could be picking up on the very last physical feelings of the supposed resident ghost, Evelyn Laye, who died of respiratory failure.* Becky also managed to point out Evelyn's image amongst a set of period photographs on the wall. The Ouija was set up and protection was put into place. Everyone's eyes focused onto the small planchette, Steve the manager joined in and looked on nervously. Suddenly Ian noticed a slight breeze over his hands, the temperature dropped and the planchette slowly moved. The planchette spelled out nonsense at first. They asked whether the spirit of Evelyn Laye could step forward. Instead of the actress, an alleged designer from Russia came forth to speak:

Becky	Did you work at this theatre?
Spirit board	'Yes'
Ian	'What year?'
Spirit board	1928
Steve	'That was the year the theatre was built.'

Fact: Amazingly this information is correct. The theatre opened in 1928. But Ian and Steve knew this fact – could automatism subconsciously cause the boys to push the planchette to the correct numbers?

Suddenly, Steve the manager asked a question. He was curious to find out more about the haunting.

Steve	'Did you try and communicate with me before?'
Spirit Board	'Yes.'
Steve	'Did you push me on the staircase?'
Spirit Board	'Yes.'
Becky	'Why do you want to make contact with Steve? Do you feel an attraction for him?'
Spirit Board	'Yes.'
Becky	'There we go again, a gay ghost!'

Becky felt the presence of another spirit; this time it was strong.

Becky	'Could you spell out your name for us please?'
Spirit Board	'E.V.E.L.Y.N.'
Becky	'Evelyn, are you resident in this theatre?'
Evelyn	'Yes.'
Steve	What is your nickname?'
The planchette spells out 'B.O.'	
Steve	'Yes, her nick name was "Boo".'

Fact: Only Steve was aware of this piece of information, therefore the power of automatism or involuntary muscular movement is divided.

Steve	'Are you responsible for the odd events that have happened in the theatre?'
Evelyn	'No'.
Ian	'Could you give us the age you died please Evelyn?'
Evelyn	'No.'
Becky	'Sounds to me like she is a real actress! A lady never gives her age!'

Conclusion   Haunted Scale: 3-10

Ian – The use of a Ouija, spirit board or talking board is a controversial subject that manages to ruffle the feathers of society. In fact, it also divides the spiritual community. In America, the boards are sold to children and perceived as nothing more than a harmless parlour game. In the United Kingdom, they are mostly seen as taboo and negative spirit conductors. Fear plays a big part in the counterproductive propaganda associated with the board. The board we see today was established during the first spiritualist movement as a conduit to spirit communication, although reports of similar boards are reported in China 500 BC. During this investigation, subconscious movement of the planchette cannot be ruled out. The Russian designer sounds legible, partly because it is so far fetched but unfortunately we cannot validate his association with the early life of the theatre. However, when the board spelt out Evelyn's nickname (even though it was spelt incorrectly) I was reasonably impressed. Stephen was the only person who knew the correct name, and it was not in his nature to push the planchette, although we can never rule out the automatisitc theory or involuntary muscular movement. With any sort of divination or planchette experiments, the risk of subconscious movement is always a possibility. At present, I remain open-minded and do not regard them as suitable channels for spirit communication. I find the tales of alleged pushing and shoving of individuals in the theatre to be circumstantial to excess psychic energy. Combine that with the myth that the building is said to be haunted by Evelyn, and without conducive proof, we naturally assume she is responsible. This haunting is probably a case of supernatural Chinese whispers.

Becky – Every form of spirit communication that I have encountered has had its drawbacks and each case is never 100 per cent accurate. I felt that the Ouija board experiment was not reliable, although it did bring up some interesting results. Spirits can read information from your aura. This could mean that 'any' spirit may have come up with the information regarding Evelyn Laye from Steve's energy field. I can confirm that no one was consciously moving the planchette. I believe the Piccadilly is haunted, possibly by the ghost of Evelyn Laye and by the gay ghost of a set designer.

The New Shakespeare's Globe

A Brief History

The area upon which the theatre is built can be traced back nearly 2,000 years to Roman London. A suburb of Londinium called *Sudwerca* (present-day Southwark) was established around the southern end of London Bridge and two major Roman roads. There have been settlements reported in the area ever since. In the Tudor and Elizabethan times, the area flourished as an entertainment district. Theatres banned from the city, by the city officials and the church, were rebuilt on the south bank as Southwark lay beyond the law makers of London. Public ale houses, bawdy houses and cock and bear-baiting arenas were plentiful. It was a favourable haunt for many pleasure seekers. There were four playhouses built in the district: the Hope, the Rose, the Swan and the Globe. The first to be built was the Rose in 1587. The Globe was built in 1597 and owned by Cuthbert Burbage. It was said to be the most magnificent theatre in London. William Shakespeare was already a household name when the theatre was built. His plays were performed at other venues in London but his best works were produced at the Globe.

Finally, in 1644, Oliver Cromwell gave his seal of approval to demolish all the theatres in London. The Globe was forgotten about for the next 350 years until 1949 when a young actor called Sam Wanamaker arrived in London. Sam wanted to rebuild a new Globe only 200 yards from the original theatre and made it his life's project. After a considerable time, and unfortunately his death, an exact replica of Shakespeare's Globe opened in 1997.

The Globe Interviews

Actress Juliet Rylance was told a ghost has been seen, 'Apparently there is an old ley line that runs through the Globe and this could be the reason a ghost was seen. A security guard that worked in the building said that he saw a Roman soldier walk across the floor right across in the direction of St Paul's Cathedral'. We later discovered the Romans did have a settlement in the area. Juliet recalls, 'Sometimes when I watched the show on the monitor backstage and you can see light and shadows moving around on the stage with the actors, it's unexplainable'. Juliet's boyfriend David appeared in *A Winter's Tale* recently and experienced something odd, 'One night after the show, I felt like I wanted to step into the tier house. But when I went in there I had a feeling like I shouldn't be there'.

Left: *Could the ghost of a boy be responsible for poltergeist activity in the wardrobe department of the Victoria Palace?*

Below: *The investigative team prepare for an all-night vigil at the Aldywch Theatre.*

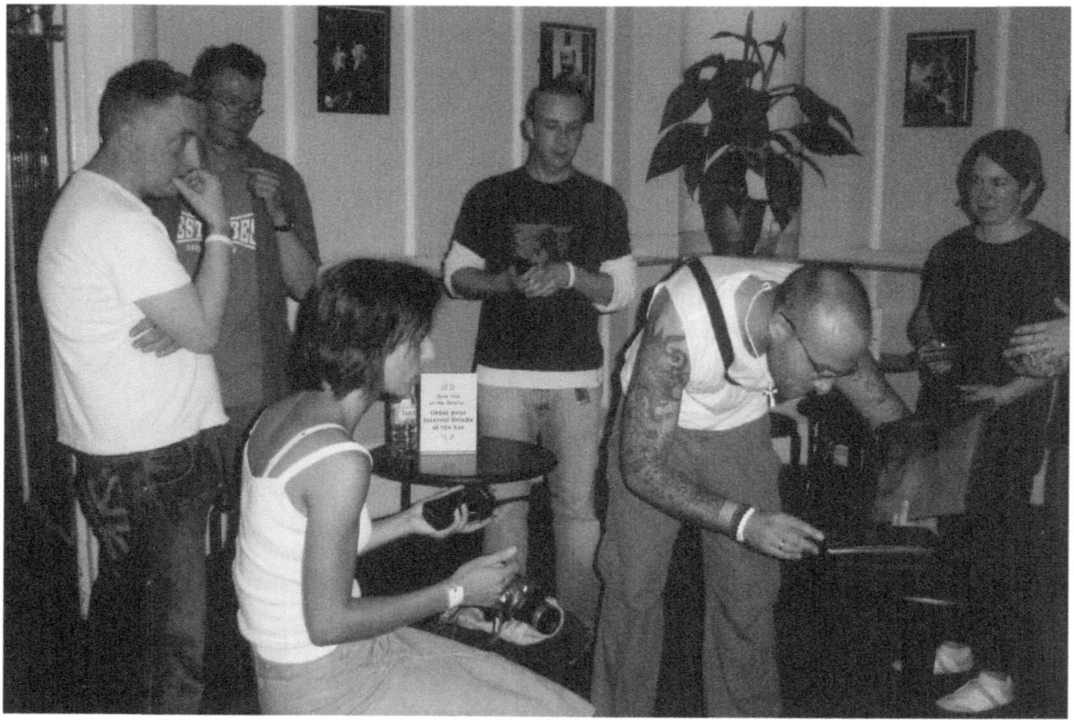

Ian and Becky delve into the residual energy underneath the stage of the Phoenix Theatre.

Is the ghost of one of the victims of the beer-vat explosion seen onstage at the Dominion Theatre?

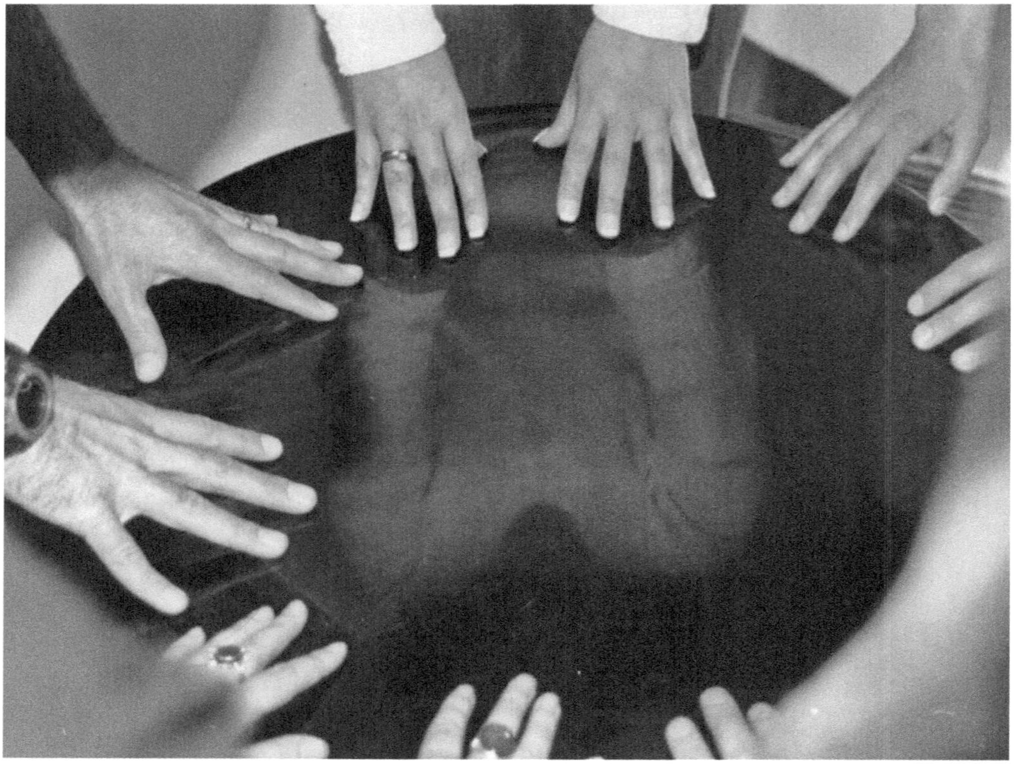

Table-tilting experiment at the Queens Theatre.

Ian captures a light anomaly at the Barbican.

A spirit overshadowing Becky or a double exposure? Box A, the Fortune Theatre.

The energy expelled from actors, lighting and machinery could result in the formation of light anomalies.

The Ghost of an Edwardian lady has been seen in the auditorium of the Dominion Theatre.

Multi-coloured orbs are seen on regular occasions at the Aldywych Theatre.

Craig Russell recalls his ghost sighting at the Queens Theatre.

Becky sits in the orchestra pit of the Dominion Theatre.

A black shadowy figure has been seen several times sub-stage at the Dominion Theatre.

The ghost of the ghost of the woman in black is spookily seen at the Fortune Theatre.

Right: *Sightings of an old theatre manager are often reported walking down this corridor at the Phoenix Theatre.*

Below: *Water droplet or spirit energy above Sandy's head.*

The team jump as they witness a red orb fly across the auditorium of the Aldwych Theatre.

A séance in the boiler room of the Trafalgar Studios.

Ian and Becky discuss the ghost of the dolphin reported to haunt under stage of the Peacock Theatre.

Gliding shadows have been witnessed by many employees at the Dominion Theatre.

The new Shakespeare's Globe

The Globe Investigation

Location: Auditorium

Reported activity: Apparition of a Roman soldier, light anomalies

Investigation: After dark, the theatre becomes a silent place yet the energy of the performance can still be felt. Becky and Ian both saw shadows moving around the stalls. Juliet declared, 'I feel that all the ancestors of theatre come and sit in the building'. Becky felt as though the team were being watched by something. The atmosphere was very strange. Becky started to see a woman wearing period clothing materialise in front of her but it suddenly disappeared as quickly as it appeared.

Location: Onstage balcony

Reported activity: None

Investigation: Ian sensed a very strong energy behind him, causing the hairs on his arm to stand on end. Amazingly, the rest of the team also felt the strange sensation on their hands. Becky made a connection, 'This is a gentleman. I feel he is connected to the theatre. He has a great sense of humour, wants to make us laugh and talks quite quickly. He is linking himself to literary things. I'm getting a name that sounds like Middleburgh or Middle something?' Juliet replied, 'The playwright, Middleton. Do you mean Thomas Middleton?' Becky agreed this could be the man and described him in detail. 'He looked like he had light hair but not quite blonde and he had a wave in it. I see him as quite big built'. Surprisingly, Becky felt Thomas was informing her that recent building work in the area is playing havoc with the natural energy from the ley line.

Conclusion   Haunted Scale: 4-10

Ian – We were extremely honoured to be allowed to investigate the theatre after dark. Once again, the residual energy left from the audience hits you like a truck. I felt residual energy and imprints played a huge role in the associated apparitions at the Globe and can explain the sighting of the Roman soldier. I was very interested in the strange lights and shadows on the show relay monitor. It could be the result of theatre lighting but I do know that the monitors are infrared. It is suggested that alleged spirit energy can manipulate our own electrical energy and therefore give one fairly possible explanation to the phenomena but a more favourable suggestion asks us to look at the spectrum of light. Infrared, along with ultraviolet light, is found beyond the scale of human sight. We all know they exist but we cannot see them. Infrared vibrates at a higher frequency to normal light and, allegedly, so does spirit energy. Like a fading cinefilm, could this piece of modern equipment actually pick up the residual stains of past inhabitants of Southwark?

After the investigation, Becky looked for an image of Thomas Middleton. When she came across an old etching, she was amazed by its similarity to the ghost she had previously encountered. Becky insists she had never seen a picture of him before. It was also discovered that Thomas had many associations with the original Globe. I felt it was possible for the spirit of Thomas to visit and communicate. Just like old ghost apparitions of the past, the spirit returned to inform us about his concern about the massive redevelopment of the area and the possible consequences it can cause. The area around the Globe has been inhabited for nearly 2,000 years. Of course it is haunted, haunted by the past and its visual outbursts.

Becky – I loved being at the Globe. It's an amazing space in its own right, even if it's not built on the original site; the foundations are still full of history. In hindsight, I wish I had concentrated more on communicating with Thomas Middleton. After researching, I was surprised to see how closely linked he was linked to the Globe Theatre. It would have been interesting to ask him whether he channels plays to any of today's playwrights. The ley line would certainly explain why there would be a lot of paranormal activity and visiting spirits in the area. Spirits are able to change their vibration on a ley line as it is a transmitter of energy.

The Duchess Theatre

Light anomalies have been reported around the backstage area. Are they connected to a sad presence which has recently been felt in one of the stairwells front of house? This fairly compact theatre was built in 1929. The majority of the stage level lays several metres below street level. Does the melancholy seep from the previous ground levels when the area was a sprawl of slums?

The Peacock Theatre

A Brief History

In 1660, Sir William D'Avenant brought the Lisle's indoor tennis court which was situated on the north side of Portugal Street, in order to build the first of many theatres on the site of the Peacock. It was rumoured to be the first ever theatre to allow women to play female characters (up to this point it was commonplace for men to play both sexes). The theatre had many names, incarnations and phases over the next 200 years. The building was used as a temporary barracks, then military head quarters for 1,400 men, an auction house and China warehouse.

In 1911, Oscar Hammerstein's London Opera House was built on the vacant plot and mirrored the elegance of the Palace of Versailles. It was a commercial disaster and closed soon after it opened. In 1970, a smaller version of the theatre was built in the bowels of a modern office block. The secluded theatre had a chequered career over the coming years. At this time, Paul Raymond produced several saucy variety shows. He installed a tank of water underneath the stage which contained two dolphins. When the tank was raised onto the stage by massive hydraulics, the dolphins were trained to remove the bikinis from the girls. Unfortunately, due to the terrible conditions and lack of light beneath the stage, the dolphins perished. Today the Peacock is a lecture theatre during the day and touring venue at night.

The Peacock Interviews

Fact or fiction, the haunting of flipper the dolphin is well known to the regular employees of the theatre. It is rumoured that the ghostly squeaks of the dolphins can be heard echoing down the backstage corridors. Spooky sounds are confirmed by one of the stage door staff. When locking up after the performances, she often hears unexplainable noises. Rather ironically, she recalls a strange phenomenon, 'I often see pools of water around the theatre. I have no idea how or where they have come from. Could this be the ghost of Flipper leaving his marks?' Another phantom has been seen many times in the past. The ghost of the wife of Oscar Hammerstein II is said to be responsible for several sightings of a lady in period clothing.

The Peacock Investigation

Location: Auditorium

Reported activity: None

Investigation: Becky surfs through the residual energy and picks up a very grand building, very different to the modern one. 'I feel there was another theatre here. It was a very grand event and full of pomp and circumstance.' The London Opera House was built over the entire block; it housed over 2,000 people and was a very grand building. Several light anomalies were witnessed by one of the team members.

Location: Sub-stage

Reported activity: Auditory phenomena

Investigation: Did Becky tune into the energy of the poor dolphins? 'I feel I'm having difficulty in breathing, I feel like I'm trapped in a place. The only way out of a situation is to die, like a prison in a way, but this is also connected with the breathing problem. Have they ever had a circus here? Just wondered if there were circus animals here? I'm feeling quite miserable down here. It's hard to pick up on where this feeling actually comes from. This space is dark and there is an overall feeling of misery'. The team felt the depression in the air; one member starts to cry. He explained, 'I am sensing real depression, loneliness and not wanting anymore, wanting to end it'. The tape recorder suddenly started to stop intermittently, even though the batteries were fully charged.

Conclusion   Haunted Scale: 1–10

Ian – The alleged haunting of Flipper the dolphin certainly made me smile. The auditory phenomenon heard within the bowels of the building is automatically linked to the poor dolphin's demise. Our natural misconceptions and understandings of haunted locations assume the animal still haunts the theatre in eternal torment. This of course is highlighted and strengthened by the

The Peacock Theatre

power of suggestion, the art of the myth and the imagination of many individuals. To be honest, most of us really want to believe the ghost of Flipper actually exists but in this case we are far beyond the truth. The only ghost here is the memory of an inhumane incident in which two animals suffered. This stain of emotion was left to fester underneath the stage. If a person with the right attributes comes along, they can instantly tune into the sadness and melancholy. This intense emotion outweighs all the previous historical facts and past personalities, causing this story to stick out like a sore thumb. This haunting verifies my belief that the darker the stain, the stronger the emotion. The alleged sounds of the suffering dolphins could be based on auditory residual energy but I feel it was more of a misdiagnosis of a natural noise. But what about the unexplained pools of water? Many theatres are built underground, close to the water table and underground rivers. Every theatre has emergency sprinkler systems. Could a leaky pipe cause the alleged watery phenomena? The theatre is laced with historical and supernatural stories but the lack of evidence proves that even though the building has all the credentials of a possible haunted location, not all theatres are haunted.

Becky – How could it be possible for a theatre to be haunted by a dolphin? Sadly, I discovered it can be possible if such horrible circumstances allow. However, I do not feel this theatre is haunted by human or mammal spirits. What happened to the poor dolphin after its death? I feel that all souls have their own evolution and animal souls evolve as a whole soul group. I feel people evolve in a more individual way. I have found through my mediumship that when we pass into the spirit world, we will meet our pets and other animals.

The Duke of York's Theatre

The theatre is rumoured to be haunted by the actress turned manager, Violet Melonette (1855–1935) whose ghost has often been seen mingling with the modern-day audience. The obscure story of 'The Strangler Jacket' originated from this theatre. The Victorian bolero jacket was used in a play in 1940. Actress Thora Hird, who wore it, complained that the garment seemed to be shrinking around her body. She found it hard to breathe even though the wardrobe mistress 'let out the seams'. Other members of the cast tried the jacket on and experienced the same reaction as did the wife of the play's director who tried it on and noticed welts appear on her throat. The jacket was eventually sold to an American collector who became very distressed when she, too, felt the strangling sensation. Incidentally, Thora Hird revealed she witnessed the ghost of a young woman in her dressing-room mirror. Rumour says the ghost and jacket belonged to a Victorian lady called Edith Merryweather, who was drowned by having her head held underwater.

The Garrick Theatre

A Brief History

During the reign of Henry VIII, the area upon which the theatre was to be built was known as the Royal Mews. The Royal or King's Mews originally contained the royal hunting birds and later developed into royal stables. During Stuart England, these buildings were used as barracks for the Parliamentary army, in which 4,500 prisoners from the Battle of Naseby were incarcerated. During 1799, Charing Cross Road was known as Castle Street. On the southernmost tip of the street, St Martin's workhouse was built on top of the old St Martin's burial ground. The workhouse was said to be the largest in the country and incorporated a parish school. In 1889, on the junction of Charing Cross Road and St Martins Lane, the Garrick Theatre was built. Due to an underground river beneath the plot, the builders had a tricky time laying foundations. The theatre was named after David Garrick, an eighteenth-century actor, playwright and theatre manager. In 1900, the theatre was managed by tragedian and comedian Arthur Bourchier who was well known in the West End.

The Garrick Interviews

If you ask any one of the Garrick's employees whether there are any particular ghost stories associated with the building, the majority will refer you to the phantom staircase. The staircase is where the ghost of Arthur Bourchier has been seen. Interestingly, Arthur died in South Africa in 1927, yet his spiritual body continues to walk the corridors of the Garrick Theatre.

Sylvia has been working on the stage door for a few years, and confirms the story of the theatre's resident spectre. She has often felt strange unexplainable breezes but senses a happy air. Sylvia recalls that Arthur's ghost was seen by Freddie Booth who was chief electrician at the theatre for forty years. Unfortunately, Freddie himself passed over a number of years ago. Freddie was apparently psychic and the ghost of Arthur seemed to make a beeline for him. One evening Freddie was walking from the manager's office and passed a man by the phantom staircase. The man was wearing a long cloak and a tall wide-brimmed hat. Freddie was stunned and only later discovered that the current manager's office used to be Arthur's dressing room.

There are countless reports of paranormal activity and Arthur seems to get the blame all the time. An usherette once fell asleep during a performance, only to suddenly awake with the feeling of a hand on her shoulder. She fled in horror.

The Garrick Theatre

Several decades ago, a stagehand witnessed the curtains rise and fall several times – no one was in the fly tower. In 1940 a strange man was seen sitting in a chair in one of the rooms front of house. He then vanished into thin air. There have been countless knocks on the box-office door over the years; everyone just assumes it is Arthur joking around.

A bottle from the bar was witnessed slowly flying through the air before crashing to the ground. Even as recently as 1980, the strange occurrences continued. During the rehearsal period of a new play the scenes kept being interrupted by a voice prompting the actors from the shadows. It actually spoke the actor's lines a split second before they did. At first this was seen as a joke, but when it carried on for several days, the company started asking questions. The resident stage management team discovered the voice was coming from the direction of the old prompt corner. No one was found responsible for the phenomenon. All this paranormal activity certainly seems to come from someone or something that likes to play a joke. Could it be Arthur Bourchier having the last laugh?

The Garrick Investigation

Location: The phantom staircase
Reported activity: Apparitions, psychic breezes
Investigation: Becky sensed a strong male energy, 'I'm picking up the energy of a comedy actor, yet I feel he has a very serous side, too. He has a responsible side to his acting work. I feel this was before World War Two'. Is this Arthur's energy? He died in 1927 and succeeded in comedy and drama. 'I feel his spirit comes back to the theatre for a reason and follows an old behavioural pattern. This theatre has such a nice feeling'.

Location: The fly floor
Reported activity: Movement of theatre curtains
Investigation: Becky suddenly noticed something move past one of the dark blue working lights. At that point Ian's camera batteries started to drain as he witnessed strange phenomena, 'Either my eyes are playing tricks on me in the dark or I am seeing movement in the shadows'.

Location: The royal box
Reported activity: None
Investigation: Becky and Ian called out to see if they could get a reaction, 'If there are any spirits here present, could you make a noise or a bang, move something and let us know that you are here?' The team notice the heavy house tabs start to move upstage and downstage rhythmically, whilst a purple haze seems to pulse over them. Ian claimed, 'It could be a breeze but there was no breeze on the fly floor'. They decided to ask it to stop. The curtains stopped. They asked it to move. They moved. 'It's like they are breathing', said Becky.

Conclusion   Haunted Scale: 3-10
Ian – The story of Arthur is a great example of a residual haunting. His ghost is like a fingerprint in time, therefore it comes as no surprise to find his imprint has been seen around the area in which he spent a considerable time. Calling the staircase 'the phantom staircase' can only manifest a legend that the staircase is home to ghosts. It encourages fear therefore creating a distribution of psychic energy tainted with anxiety. The layman can come into this room which the knowledge that it is supposedly haunted and automatically sense the stain of nervousness left by other people, therefore enhancing the story further. As I am interested in actual physical phenomena, I was at first excited to see the pulsing curtains and mysterious haze. However, in the light of day, I felt it was not supernatural. Even though they moved on command, we could not discount natural air flow in the building. The source of the haze was a challenge at first because the lighting rig was switched off. I think the power of suggestion is a possible explanation to the alleged activity. Becky reported she could see a purple glow on the curtains; a second later so could I. During investigations our minds naturally open up and read into many things we normally ignore. In the heat of the moment, even though we all try to remain rational, it is easy to confuse imagination, reality and non-reality.

Becky – I felt the theatre was unusually quiet and I wish we had discovered more phenomena. The phantom staircase sounds very spooky, but to be honest I believe it to be only a name. It just goes to show that, no matter how many ghost stories are associated with the theatre, I feel most of them are exaggerated by the West End jungle drums. Is the theatre haunted? I don't think so. I tuned into the residual energy of Arthur Bourchier and not his spirit. The energy within the building is full of love and it was pleasure to feel it.

Sadler's Wells

In 1683, Richard Sadler built the first of six theatres to be erected on the site. During the 1800s Joseph Grimaldi appeared on stage at the Theatre Royal Drury Lane before running several miles across London to appear at Sadler's Wells later that evening. Joseph was most famous for his creation of 'Joey the Clown'. Not only one of the resident ghosts at the lane, it seems there is also a report that the ghost of 'Grimaldi the Clown' was seen in one of the boxes in Sadler's Wells over 200 years after his death. We have to ask, if his ghost is only a residual replay, why would he be seen in a box watching the show and not onstage or backstage? Maybe his energy has returned to view the many different theatres built on this site.

The Prince of Wales Theatre

A man dressed in a grey coat is said to walk the stage left wing. Could this be the old actor manager Edgar Bruce who worked at the theatre in 1884? It seems that a vast majority of alleged sightings and stories we looked at are all associated with the old actor-managers.

The Playhouse Theatre

A Brief History
The site of the Playhouse Theatre can be traced as far back as 1450. The area was originally the grounds of St Mary Rounceval, an Augustinian hospital for the poor. By 1737, on the site of the theatre a huge timber yard endlessly supplied building materials. A century later the yard closed due land clearance for the building of Charing Cross Station. In 1882, the Royal Avenue Theatre was built on land put aside for the expansion of the station.

On 5 December 1905, the roof of the neighbouring Charing Cross Station suddenly collapsed, sending twenty to thirty workmen plummeting to the ground. The incident caused a major wall which backed on the Playhouse to thrust backwards, raining debris into the theatre and down onto the stage. Many were injured in the collapse but luckily only six men died, two of whom were working in the theatre. Unfortunately, because of the complete size of the disaster, several of the bodies were trapped under the debris for several days. Alfred Burch and Thomas Richards, who sadly perished, were working in the theatre. In *The Times* newspaper that week, it was said to be the most appalling accident in London of that time and was labelled 'The Charing Cross disaster'.

The theatre was rebuilt and opened again for business in 1907. In 1933 it changed its name to the Playhouse Theatre and carried on producing and showing plays until the early 1950s.

The Playhouse Investigation
Location: Auditorium
Reported activity: None
Investigation: Both Ian and Becky sensed a mysterious energy that seemed to push them to one side. Becky asked:

> Did something collapse? I'm getting the feeling that something fell in? When it fell in there was shock wave, I get the impression of lots of choking dust. People were crushed to death as a result. I can see people pushing and shouting, like a mass evacuation. Sadly, I felt someone died underneath all the rubble but their body was recovered days later. Sadly, I felt they didn't die straight away, they were unconscious but still alive.

Was Becky tuning into the collapse of the station's roof? The team decided to experiment with a form of scrying to evoke any paranormal activity. They looked into the eyes of two gilded heads built into one of the theatres boxes. Surprisingly, the plaster faces seemed to look back. Everyone in the team noticed what appeared to be a slight glow and the eyes seemed the move. It was a

The Playhouse Theatre

little daunting. Becky declared, 'I'm getting a man in his mid-twenties with a long face, I can see tension in the jaw'. Two of the men killed in the 1905 tragedy were in their twenties.

Conclusion   Haunted Scale: 0.5–10

Ian – This particular investigation just goes to show that the stain of a past horrific event may not necessarily blend into the present ether. The energy from the Charing Cross disaster and the unfortunate deaths were picked up by Becky's psychic ability, but more importantly failed to express itself as a possible residual haunting as we could find no reported sightings. The lack of phenomena found at The Playhouse could possibly explain the reasons to why the believer and science fail to supply concrete evidence when trying to uncover the causes behind paranormal activity. They can only suggest and make claims within their own understanding. This theory underlines my belief that ghost and paranormal investigations are exactly what they say they are, investigations into the sub-normal and supernatural with no conceivable endings. I feel we are never fully meant to understand this, and our curious questioning only enhances the natural development of our physical, mental and spiritual self.

The scrying experiment, even though we all thought we witnessed the eyes move and face change, was not conducive of paranormal activity. On this occasion, I felt our minds tried to interpret what we were all hoping to see. We all wanted to see the static face move. We subconsciously sent out a thought to witness it and 'as if by magic', we started to notice movement. I also felt the power of suggestion played a huge role. However, Becky did manage to sense a young man whose description could have matched one of the poor lads who died in the disaster. I felt that was Becky tuning into the residual stain of the boy's character.

Becky – I don't believe the Playhouse Theatre is haunted, despite the unfortunate disaster that happened, although the residual energy was reasonably strong. I felt that there were no spirits trapped or grounded and those that died passed into the light naturally. Scrying has been used for many years as a focus for clairvoyant sight. Staring into an object (usually a crystal ball but can be applied in other ways) allows the mind to become a canvas for any psychic impressions you may receive. The transfiguration of the gold face ornament could be put down to our eyes playing tricks. I do not think there was enough evidence to say it was paranormal.

The London Coliseum

A classic residual haunting is said to be the cause of odd sensations in the building. The ghost of a soldier form the First World War has been seen walking in the auditorium prior to a performance. The story recalls that the soldier had spent his last night of leave at the theatre and was later killed in action. However, his apparition has not been seen since for eighty-five years. It is also suggested that the balcony of the auditorium is haunted by a former housekeeper who manifests herself as a lady in black. Once again, this has all the signs of a residual haunting.

The Vaudeville Theatre

A Brief History
In 1682, a maze of alleys and small dark courtyards were previously built on the site of the former Vaudeville Theatre. Oliver's alley, Sheerman's Entry, Bulle Inn and Lumley Alley (Lumley Street and Bull Inn still exist today) divided the large expanse of tenements that studded the Strand. Through the seventeenth and eigtheenth centuries, the area was renowned for crime and the alleys leading off the Strand were favourite haunts of pickpockets and prostitutes. In 1869, William Robertson built a theatre on the site of his failed billiards club. Producing mostly revue and vaudeville shows, this was to be the first incarnation of the Vaudeville theatre. In 1900-1906, the great impresario Seymour Hicks and his wife Ella line Terris, acted in a series of long runs. (You may remember Seymour from the Aldwych Theatre investigation.) The Vaudeville had a difficult time during its first decades; the building was closed and refurbished three times. Each theatre has managed to retain a substantial part of the previous building. Beneath the current stage, several of the original traps still survive. Backstage, an early leather thunder drum and lightening sheet, used for sound effects, still exists, and above the stage in the Grid the original timbered machinery reminds us all of the theatre's history.

The Vaudeville Interviews
The shadows of the Vaudeville Theatre are said to be the home of a regular apparition yet no one knows who it is. Alistair Sutherland the theatre manager has confirmed there have been a number of paranormal things happening recently. Damien Parker has worked in the box office for twenty-five years. He is an open-mined sceptic, yet he has often experienced an unexplainable smell. He regularly smells ladies' perfume around the building. Damien is convinced it smells very old-fashioned as it does not seem to have that modern aroma. He is insistent that there is a

The Vaudeville Theatre

presence in the building as sometimes he feels as though he is being watched. Damien informs us that he believes the ghost is female.

One unfortunate employee was working in the bar one evening and realised she was out of ice. In those days, the ice machine was kept in the cellar. As she filled up her ice bucket, she felt the temperature drop; it had never been that cold before. All of a sudden a cold hand touched her on her shoulder; she jumped and turned around. No one was there. One day after the show, a pest control man was in the same cellar setting traps. Knowing he was the only one left in the theatre, he was shocked to see a woman walk around one of the corners in the small cellar. He managed to notice that she was wearing a long black cloak before the apparition disappeared into thin air. He was so frightened he left the theatre immediately. There is one rumour that several secret tunnels run under the Strand and down to the Thames. Could this be where the ghosts are hiding?

The Vaudeville Investigation

Location: Foyer

Reported activity: None

Investigation: 'I'm sensing a Victorian woman', said Becky. 'She is wearing a long layered skirt, and the fabric is course with a heavy weave. I believe she wore three layers underneath her skirt. This lady looked a little rough around the edges, I feel as if she was a prostitute, a lady of the night. She also wore a small bonnet on the side of her head. I can see her running down an alley; this image is so clear I could even draw her for you'. There are many references to prostitution in the history of the area. During the nineteenth century, the site of the theatre and the surrounding alleys and courtyards had become a terrible red-light district. Suddenly, Ian became aware of a man's energy behind him. Becky could see the vibration and was excited, 'He is a strong chap, tall and well built; I'm convinced we have seen him before. He is tall, just under 6ft, and curiously wore boots with a heel. He walks in a grand way with his head high. He definitely has a link to the theatres; it's as if he had a production company who had several shows on in the West End'. Ian felt this energy was Seymour Hicks as his description fitted perfectly.

Location: Cellar
Reported activity: Apparition of a cloaked lady, cold spots
Investigation: Becky immediately tuned into something, 'I feel someone was pulled down here via the barrel run, and murdered; I felt as if they had their throat slit. They were left here and found in the morning. It's a horrible feeling'. Unexpectedly there was a sound of two bottles banging together. The team jumped. How can this be? One of the rooms is full of crates of beer. They were alone, or were they?

Location: Office stairwell
Reported activity: None
Investigation: This stairwell was originally used as an exit for the lower classes. Becky grabbed her throat, 'I have a very hot feeling round my neck, which feels like hot hands. I feel like the blood is trapped in my head. I feel as if I can't breath. I felt there was a woman strangled here. She was dragged up these stairs. I feel there is a door round this corner and the man was trying to drag her through that door'. Ian walks around the corner and discovers there is a door to the gent's toilet.

Conclusion   Haunted Scale: 4-10
Ian – If I was to make assumptions on the collected evidence from Becky's walk around and witness sightings, I would presume the alleged ghost of the woman would be the spectre of a murdered prostitute. A murder is often seen as a perfect cause for a haunting although I feel the story a little obvious. However, we do have to look at the historical facts. The area was infamous for prostitution and the alleyways that lead off the busy Strand harboured many undesirables. A murder or attack may have happened and not been reported although I found that hard to swallow. Psychics can tune into leftover residual energy of the traumatic event and relive those last emanations; however, they can also read other information associated with the characters. Names, dates and other relevant information can also be picked up in a kind of high definition residual chalkboard. This can often be misinterpreted as actual spirit communication. Becky agrees that she was only sensing the very first layer of residual. The very brief noises in the cellar could be natural but it is not confirmed. They definitely came from another room in the cellar and I can guarantee we were completely alone. I felt this theatre deserved another investigation and had all the possible hallmarks of a haunted theatre.

Becky – The amount of energy and strong feelings in this theatre were very intense. The feeling of strangulation I experienced on the stairwell was also very strong. I was not sure whether it was actually spirit hands around my neck or the impression of the past attack. When I asked for that feeling to be removed, it was, thus confirming it was only residual energy. It was a complete joy to discover the identity of the man was who had been following us on other investigations. Ian is 95 per cent convinced it was Seymour Hicks. Although we can never give 100 per cent validation, the descriptions fit perfectly.

The Lyric Theatre

The Lyric Theatre was built in 1888. Previously, the site was occupied by the home and museum of the eighteenth-century anatomist Dr William Hunter. The museum and adjoining anatomy theatre were demolished in order to build the resident dressing rooms. It is known that many of the dissected cadavers were supplied illegally by body snatchers. Do the dressing rooms of the Lyric Theatre still hold the energies of those unfortunate few who ended up on the dissection table?

The theatre is also reported to be haunted by a more recent ghost. The spirit of murdered programme seller Nellie Klute has been associated with this building. Is this story referring to the same person as the ghost of an usher who was killed in the First World War by a Zeppelin's bomb? The spectral figure is seen gliding down the aisles.

The Theatre Royal Haymarket

A Brief History

Back in 1513 on the site of the theatre, John Norris and his wife lived in their croft surrounded by 3 acres of fields. In 1575, the widow Golightly brought the land at a reasonable price as the area was not necessarily pretty, due to the approaching threat and smell of the city of London. In 1720, a small theatre was commissioned to be built on the site of the Kings Head Inn and a small gun-makers shop. Simply called The Little Theatre, it ran for seventeen years before getting into debt. In 1767, the building was expanded and given its new name, The Theatre Royal. One evening in 1794, disaster struck. The king was in attendance during a performance when a large crowd pushed forward in order to capture a glimpse of him. A riot broke out causing twenty people to lose their lives and many to be injured. Finally in 1821 and under new management the theatre opened to a production of *The Rivals*. David Edward Morris was the new manager and continued to be until the mid-1880s. The most successful manager at this theatre was John Baldwin Buckstone, a popular actor and comedian. Today, the Theatre Royal Haymarket has achieved considerable success since its official start nearly 300 years ago.

The Haymarket Interviews

The theatre has had multiple sightings of one individual and many solid manifestations. Past employees have witnessed shadows and heard strange noises. In the Theatre Royal Haymarket, you are never alone.

In his lifetime, John Buckstone was a feather in the cap of the theatre. He was the blue-eyed boy. In death, he is a spectral celebrity; his frequent appearances probably make him the most seen ghost in the West End. Within a year of his passing, his ghost was seen in the Royal Box viewing the resident show. Buckstone lived in a house attached to the back of the theatre which is now occupied by the building's offices and dressing rooms. The ghost of Buckstone seems to have free range throughout the theatre. A ghostly apparition fitting Buckstone's description has been seen in dressing rooms, on the stairwells and, once, actually onstage in a performance.

One of the most active areas seems to centre on dressing room 1, and according to rumour this was Buckstone's dressing room. Since his passing, fellow actors who had resided in the room have heard rummaging from empty cupboards, a man's voice or footsteps coming from inside the room. Doors have been witnessed opening and closing. Many years ago a ghost hunter stayed the night; he was drawn to the dressing room when he, too, heard rustling from within, and

The Theatre Royal, Haymarket

when he opened the door he noticed a book lying open on a table with the pages turning over by themselves. The late Margaret Rutherford and her husband once stayed the night in his old dressing room. During the night they awoke to hear strange creaking noises coming from the direction of the bricked-up doorway. The doorway used to be Buckstone's personal entrance to the stage. The following evening, Margaret and her dresser were convinced they saw him entering her dressing room. A high-calibre theatre like the Haymarket brings high-calibre actors to the building. They, too, have seen Buckstone's ghost.

Dame Judi Dench, recounted her story to Becky:

I was talking part in the late Michael Dennison's memorial service, which was held at the Theatre Royal Haymarket. At the time, I did not know of any ghosts at the theatre, but I believe there are several. I was on my way from the stage to the auditorium and, just in front of me, I saw a man in a long tailcoat run ahead of me along a corridor. He did not look like the impression we all have of ghosts, and I just thought he was another guest who was strangely dressed. When I reached the end of the corridor and turned the corner, he had completely disappeared.

Sir Donald Sinden CBE experienced a similar occurrence to Ian:

It was 1949, and I was making my West End debut in a production of *The Heiress* with Ralph Richardson. I was walking from my dressing room to the stage with my colleague, Gillian Howell, when we noticed who we thought was Ralph in his 1860 period costume, standing by his dressing room deep in thought and looking out of the window. We both said 'Good Evening' and thought nothing of it when he didn't reply. We carried on towards the stage, gossiping, then suddenly stopped in our tracks when we realised at that moment Ralph was onstage. I quickly ran back up the stairs but the man was gone.

Ian   'Can you explain what he was wearing?'
Donald   'He was in a dark grey frockcoat, like a mourning coat. He definitely looked Victorian.'
Ian   'Donald, can I ask are you are a believer or do you think it's all a load of non-sense?'
Donald   'I think it's a load of nonsense, although it doesn't explain why I saw a ghost.'

Sir Donald was full of beans retelling this story. He remembered another ghostly event at a now-defunct St James Theatre. A horrifying laugh echoed around the stage at the same time in a play for three consecutive nights, culminating in a bloodcurdling scream. There was no reasonable explanation. It terrifies him to this day.

Tony is the master carpenter at the Haymarket, and retold his story at the start of our investigation.

One night, at the end of a show, when I was taking the house tabs out, I turned round and saw a guy stood by the door. The man was dressed in an old cloak and top hat; he had chubby cheeks. I knew every body had left the building and I was alone. I thought it was an actor from another theatre.

Tony explains that he immediately knew he was looking face to face at a ghost. 'The ghost did not look like I'd imagined; it wasn't transparent in a "floaty" way. I went to talk to him, but suddenly he just disappeared – he wasn't see-through. I was so scared, I had a heartbeat in my head. I had a headache for days'. Tony said, he did not tell anyone for months, but then finally plucked up the courage to inform his sister, who then told the then deputy master carpenter.

'I had only been here a year and didn't know about the ghost. The deputy master carpenter took me to the theatre archives and said "Open that book up and you will see him in there" and the picture was exactly how he was, even down to his chubby cheeks.' Tony was shown a photograph of the old actor/manager John Buckstone, whose ghost was said to walk the theatre. Tony shows us a bricked-up doorway in the stage right wing, and a place of the apparition. 'This is his doorway from his dressing room. He was happy, he was smiling; he wasn't like the sort of ghost you would expect'. Tony explains that this is not the only paranormal thing he has witnessed at the theatre:

I stay overnight here a lot, and some nights you here nothing, but on others you here people on stage. I have to come up and check, just in case someone has broken in, there is never anyone there. I don't think it's a ghost but when I go to sleep, I turn the sound up on the television, so I can't hear it.

The ghost of another manager is also said to retrace his steps, but this time his aura is not so sweet. Every few years, the ghost David Edward Morris is said to put in a regular appearance. In life, he was reported to be a jealous, quarrelsome and a pompous individual. Morris is said to open and close doors in front of unsuspecting victims in a ghostly joke. There seems to be a little bit of a confusion regarding who the apparitions in the theatre actually are. Some stories say it is Buckstone, some say Morris and others have Henry Fielding as another suspect. However, when the majority of witnesses are shown a photograph of Buckstone, they confirm it was him they saw.

Another ghost that has been seen at the theatre is that of an elderly man who walks silently down the passages of backstage. This spook likes to haunt the oldest parts of the building, especially near one of the boxes. One managing director noticed not one, but two shadows following her; one was her own, the other carried on gliding past when she stopped walking. Could it be the spectral form of the lady seen in the wardrobe? Or maybe one of the unfortunate victims who were trampled to death by the audience riot of 1794?

Brian Russell has been a stage door man at the Haymarket for twenty-one years. Up until recently, he classed himself a sceptic, and had never seen or heard anything paranormal at the theatre. He said he was aware of the history and the alleged ghosts, but never came across one until he was down underneath the stage one evening, 'I was turning off the lights when all of a sudden I walked through what can be only described as an electrical energy. So strong was this energy, it turned my stomach'.

Walking into the Haymarket will be like walking through a quagmire of historical and supernatural flotsam and jetsam.

The Haymarket Investigation

Location: Onstage by bricked-up doorway

Reported activity: Regular apparitions of a Victorian gentleman

Investigation: Becky allowed herself to tune into the energy in a trance-like state and spoke on behalf of the alleged ghost, 'Am I on trial? A breed apart – that of the actor and that of the technician. You could be working on a building site. Not many actors have any credibility in behind what they do; I find many of the stage productions here appalling. It's not a case of not what they used to be – there is no art behind the roles, the characters are lacking, and the direction is shoddy. I find it quite disgusting'.

Location: Dressing room 1

Reported activity: Regular apparitions of a Victorian gentleman, poltergeist activity, auditory phenomena

Investigation: Becky described a man, 'I feel this would have been quite tall and broad across the shoulders. So with his hat on, he would have looked very big'. Interestingly the lights flickered. 'He is a big bloke! Really big, 6ft in height, grey coat, and his shoulders are padded; I want to put my hand forward, as if I am holding a cane'. The team felt the air becoming colder as Ian tuned into the energy, 'He sits forward on his cane. He has many of the young actresses in this room talking to them and flirting with them. I feel that he would be a man who could hire them and keep them in work. I sense the ladies in different stages of undress as they talk to him. They would come in to see him without the large dresses and costumes, like most actors do when they come offstage in uncomfortable clothes. He's a real story teller'.

Conclusion   Haunted Scale: 10-10

Ian – Most people who work in the West End claim that the Theatre Royal Drury Lane is the most haunted theatre in the district, however I tend to differ. If we are looking at actual paranormal sightings and phenomena associated within the buildings, the Theatre Royal Haymarket wins by far. The activity far outweighs the stories at The Lane. The fact that the ghost of John Buckstone is as famous now as he was when he was alive is a shining example of a thought from haunting. Residually, I felt that the image of Buckstone may well have been seen on numerous occasions in the past. This evolved into a legend-size story and therefore brought further thought and energy into the present. As this energy multiplied over the years, so did the belief that this particular phantom was him. Or was it? Bear in mind, in Buckstone's day, most men who came to the theatre dressed very similarly so the residual replay could be anyone of those. Whatever the outcome and I doubt there is a correct explanation, the idea that the building is haunted by such a wonderful and caring character can only enhance the superstition in the theatre. When Becky entered a trance-like state, I felt she was tuning into leftover residual energy rather than a spirit actually talking through her. It was interesting that the character seemed to be quite in support of the actor/technician divide but I felt that the alleged spirit failed to inform me of any sufficient information that I could later validate, therefore I felt the communication came from the distillation of Becky's higher self and the residual history. I am fascinated with the stories associated with this theatre and would love to come back for an overnight vigil.

Becky – Normally, I wouldn't be happy letting a spirit talk through my mouth. Being somewhat of a control freak, I have always found trance an odd thing to do, but once you realise you are in complete control, it becomes very easy. We wanted to investigate the Haymarket ever since we received contact from Dame Judi Dench and Sir Donald Sinden. The ghost of John Buckstone has been seen by many people; many of these are well known in the public eye. This theatre is defiantly the most haunted theatre we have investigated. It is also one of the most beautiful theatres in the West End. It truly is a stunning theatre full of history and phantoms.

Summary

Ian – If there is one thing I have deducted from this series of investigations is that there is not one single conceivable explanation for a ghost sighting or paranormal activity. Whether it is residual, grounded, poltergeist, psychic energy, a thought form, a time-slip or visitation, the alleged phenomena could be the result of an aspect of all these conditions. The biggest cause of paranormal activity is of course the power of the mind and the power of thought, be that subconscious or intentional, negative or positive. Fear is also one of the major factors which fans the flames of myth, legend and belief. Not understanding our fears can cause the fear to multiply, which in term forces our rational mind to hibernate.

I am truly amazed by the results both Becky and I have discovered. All the theatrical characters (both living and dead) have enlightened me greatly. We have deduced that it is possible to reconstruct and illuminate the past with perceived psychic interpretations. History and its past are also essential to our own identities. If we did not have the past we would not have the present, let alone the future. Psychics and mediums can only suggest the possibility of life after death by giving evidence not proof. Some say we will never know the outcome. I feel the truth behind the paranormal will always remain unanswered.

I'm happy we decided to concentrate on the lesser-known theatres as opposed to the obvious choices. It made our journey a journey into the unknown. Out of all the theatres we investigated we both felt The Theatre Royal Haymarket was the most haunted (in the old sense of the word) with The Victoria Apollo and Fortune Theatre following a close second. Only a few theatres missed our hit list: the Wyndams, Apollo, Criterion, National and Gielgud theatres remain silent. We could not find one single story or reference to paranormal activity associated with any one of these theatres even though we scratched away at the surface. When I examined the alleged haunting and stories associated with the West End, it never ceased to amaze me how quickly one can justify them in the light of day, yet in the midst of action they all appear so plausible. This book just goes to show that the ghost is never far away and paranormal activity can be part of everyday life. It's just a case of looking in all the right places.

Writing this book has been a very cathartic exercise. It has reintroduced me to the wonder and magical world of theatre, a feeling that I first experienced in my youth and something I had since forgotten about. All the show palaces, with their grandeur and grime and panto and Pinter have impressed me far beyond words. I am honoured to be part of this massive and very important department of society. Theatre ghosts have laced together two very important but contrasting interests in my life. My spiritual side and my past theatrical side have finally joined as one, be that for a short moment only. My theatrical career has run its course and my passion for the paranormal has ignited a vibrant flame. I will never forget this experience.

Becky – When one goes on a ghost hunt or recounts a ghost story, it is easy to forget that the ghost or energy was an actual living person with a physical body. We neglect the fact that it lived and breathed on this earth plane. Most of us interpret a ghost as a fearful apparition which is stuck in time. We see their non-psychical life stranded between the planes of existence, where the occupation of their body has ended. I think this interpretation is one of the reasons why ghosts can appear so scary. This belief enforces us to not see them as people like you and me but as an apparition, a spectre, a phantom stuck between the two worlds in eternal torment. If we saw the ghost as a fully manifested spirit in solid form, just like you and me, the chances are we would not run for the hills. It is my belief that the mystery which surrounds the ghost and paranormal is mainly the cause of our fear.

One thing that was confirmed on our journey across the West End is that the energy of life can go on transformed and immortalised forever in the very walls and foundations of buildings. An actor can put on a costume, walk the stage and immediately transport us to a moment in time, a moment in history. Sensing energy can do the same. Psychics use their clairvoyant skills to see, hear and sense the past.

Are the theatres haunted? Are the ghosts real? I feel there are energies present, though they are few and far between. I feel in some aspect their life goes on and their involvement in the theatre is still present in the here and now. However, I do feel that many theatrical characters who have successfully transformed their energy from a physical being to a spirit being also pop back from time to time. I feel their message is very clear. It informs us of the simple fact not to fear death. Spirit informs us that there is no end and after the death of the physical body, the play of life goes on for eternity.

In this book, I hope we have helped you reach a similar notion and passed on this message successfully. This merry dance of life has many partners, all of whom you will meet again in the spirit world and get the chance to dance again.

I like to compare our physical life to a play. Whether comedy or tragedy, short or long in length, we know it cannot last forever. So let us enjoy it whilst it it's here. Whatever the reviews, whatever we experience, one thing we must remind ourselves it that there is always a cracking after show party just around the corner.

BIBLIOGRAPHY

London Theatres and Music Halls 1850-1950, Diana Howard, the Library Association
The Theatres of London, Raymond Mander and Joe Mitchenson, New English Library
The London Encyclopaedia, Ben Web and Christopher Hibbert, Macmillan
The London Stage 1576-1888, H.B. Baker
Great Theatres of London, Ronald Bergan
1700 Scenes from London Life, Maureen Waller, Four Walls Eight Windows
Psychic Protection, Judi Hall
Dancing with the Devil, David Ashworth

To contact Ian www.londonparanormalsociety.co.uk.
To contact Becky www.lightofspirit.co.uk.
Also by Becky Walsh, *Advanced Psychic Development*, O Books.